Scratching For Wisdom

By

Alec Gould

© 2025 by Alec Gould All rights reserved. Copyright under Berne Copyright Convention, Universal Copyright Convention, and Pan-American Copyright Convention. No part of this book may be reproduced, stored in a retrieval system, or transmitted in any form, or by any means, electronic, mechanical, photocopying, recording or otherwise, without prior permission of the author.

A JumpingCatPublication

978-1-7364564-4-6

More great books to read, by Alec Gould:

- **When You Hear Meow**
- **We Really Need To Laugh**
- **Ploop**
- **Ted-D's Happy, Sad, Birthday Day**
- **Eternal Sin – The L.A. Story**
- **Kruser's Point of View**

Www.AlecGould.com

Alec Gould. com

I would like to offer my thanks to those in my life whom, without their belief in me, this book would not have been written, nor any of my other books.

***

My editor and partner in life, the woman I have known for over 44 years, and having spent a better share of it together, Gloria, who is also known as Alicia. Yes, she has a pen name, too. With her belief in me and her editing skills, turns my words into a format in which my readers enjoy. Thank you, Love. For always being there, even in those times in which I have had too much caffeine and continue to talk at length.

Brenda, my fellow sax player and good friend. She has a belief in me which is also priceless. Not only that, but she is known to step up to the plate and help with editing. Without her help, "When You Hear Meow" may have taken a bit longer to write. Thank you, buddy! As Boots Randolph always told me, "Keep on honkin'."

Sheri, an avid reader and friend who helps me in my financial aspects. I'm glad she also looks forward to my next book, no matter what the subject matter may be.

To Ted-D for always helping me get the words on the page and helping with topics. Thanks Ted-D. You make life so much easier to "bear."

Boo-Boo, Nellie, Yogie, and Marbles. You help me get up each day, either by putting your butts on my face or hacking just a wee bit louder in order to wake me up for the morning hairball. I appreciate each one of you and could not imagine life without each of you in it.

Lastly, Alec-the-Cat. The cornerstone of these stories. In spirit, as in life, she is my guiding light. When I look up into the night sky, that last star on Orion's belt twinkles for something not many would understand. Thank you, Alec buddy. I miss you but know you are always nearby.

Encore. Yes. Encore. To all my readers. For enjoying my stories, my books. And for your patience and understanding of this past year of my life. Thank you for being here for me and also for each of your emails. I enjoy them all and always try to answer each one. If you don't hear from me, write again, and I will send you an apology for somehow missing you. You are each individually important in my life. I appreciate each one of you. Thank you!

This story, although good on its own, continues from the first book "When You Hear Meow", from Ted-D's and the kitty's - Nellie, Marbles, Yogie, and Boo-Boo - points of view, mostly.

Enjoy. . .

***

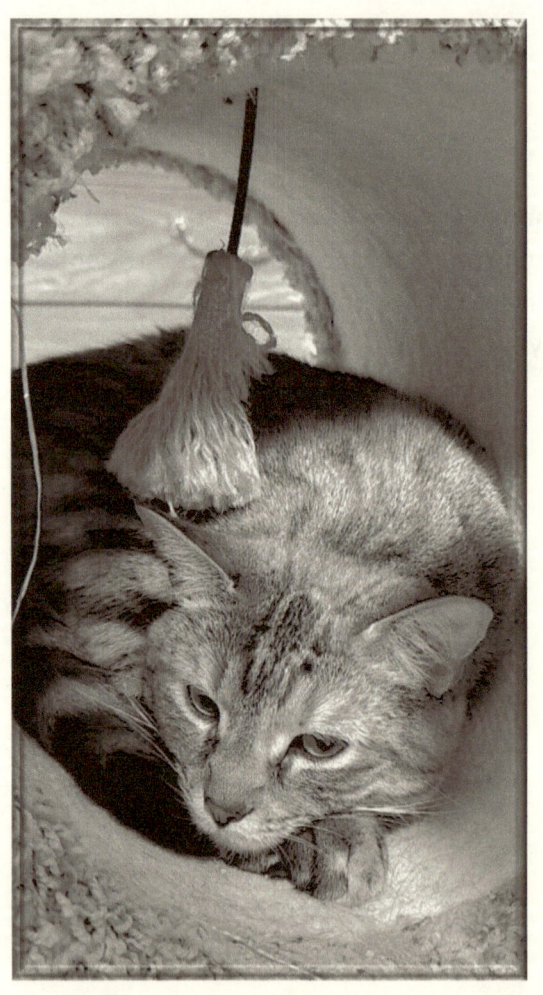

MEW 1	15
MEW 2	25
MEW 3	37
MEW 4	41
MEW 5	49
MEW 6	55
MEW 7	59
MEW 8	67
MEW 9	71
MEW 10	77
MEW 11	83
MEW 12	91
MEW 13	95
MEW 14	97
MEW 15	105
MEW 16	109
MEW 17	113
MEW 18	121
MEW 19	123
MEW 20	131
MEW 21	139
Mew 22	145
MEW 23	151
MEW 24	157

MEW 25 163
MEW 26 167
MEW 27 171

MEW 1

Another new day was just beginning for the kittens. Yes, it was shortly after one in the afternoon, but as I had stated, KITTENS. As we all know, kittens and kitties, cats and fur buddies are one and the same, and so they get up or sleep whenever they wish. So, as I had stated, the new day was just beginning for the kittens.

Not much is known prior to their birth in July, but we do know they have been a wonderful group of sisters for their foster parents since they arrived. And since they were just born in July, every day was going to be a new day for them, at least for their first year.

They were originally a litter of six, all girls, but two of their sisters had been adopted, leaving the four of them to enjoy one another until they would be adopted out too. Until then, they explored their home of many corners and get much needed, yes, much needed and deserving, pets.

The sun shone brightly in the window, only to be stopped by Marbles, the larger of the four, before it could complete its 92.49-million-mile trip to the carpet of the living room where they played. Marbles did not care as she warmed in its rays of luxury. As she did, her sisters, Nellie and Boo-Boo, played with the balls which were on a circled tower, batting them with their paws in awe of how the balls returned to them so they could repeat it all over again. Almost like humans bowling, these balls kept returning to them in their delight. Yogie, the quietest of them all, laid in Winston's lap, receiving pets and belly rubs. She herself felt protected from the world with him. Life seemed good until the ringing of the doorbell. The girls scurried under the table for safety, including Yogie who leapt from Winston's lap. Winston chuckled.

"It's all right, girls," he said. "It's alright. Only the doorbell. Probably your new parents."

Karen went to the door to see who had scared her feline little friends. "Yes, it's your new parents. I sure hope they are as nice in person as they were on the phone and email." As she did with each adoptive parent throughout the years, she opened the door in apprehension. "You must be Gloria and, oh, I am so sorry, I forgot your name."

Gloria inserted the missing name, "Don. Yes, it is us." Gloria smiled and was greeted with a return one from Karen.

"Don, yes, Don. I never talked with you, so please excuse my forgetfulness. Won't you please come in?" Opening the door further, Karen left them in with a sweep of her arm. Seeing Don busy at the door she stated, "No, no, you are quite all right leaving your shoes on. No need to fuss. Please come in and meet my husband and the girls, as we like to call the kitties."

Going around the couch to be introduced to Winston, Don and Gloria were careful where they stepped.

"Yes, the girls do have a lot of toys to keep them busy. We find it keeps them from chewing or playing with the curtains and other items they should not be playing with."

Gloria agreed, "I understand. I've had many cats in my life, and yes, they do need to be kept occupied." She smiled warmly at their hostess.

"My name is Ted-D," came the words from Don's pocket. Ted-D peeked out.

"Yes, yes, this here is Ted-D," Gloria said. "Sorry, Ted-D. We should have introduced you right away."

"That's OK, Momma. But I couldn't wait no more. I am so excited to meet my sisters," Ted-D said with eyes so big.

"Well, hello Ted-D," Karen said reaching out her hand to shake Ted-D's paw. "I am so glad to meet you."

Ted-D shook Karen's hand. "I am so glad to meet you, too. Can I go on the floor and see my new sisters?"

"Why, of course you can, Ted-D. That is, if it is alright with your parents." Karen looked at Don and Gloria.

"Of course, buddy." Don said as Gloria nodded yes. Putting Ted-D down on the floor Don continued, "Now, take it slow Ted-D. We don't want to scare the little ones, us being strangers to them yet."

"I'll take it slow, Daddy." Ted-D said. He slowly got down on his belly, butt in the air and started crawling towards Marbles who was under the table with her sisters. The adults grinned ear to ear.

"He's going to be a very good brother to the girls. I can see that already," Winston said in his low voice, a chuckle followed.

As Don made small talk with Winston about the football game on the television, Karen and Gloria's eyes were watching Ted-D with the kittens.

"It looks like they are getting along well already."

Behind the tablecloth, which hung low, the girls spied a look at Don and Gloria.

"I don't know if I like this, Marbles." It was Yogie, the shy one, who spoke.

Yogie and her sisters waited for Marbles to reply. Marbles, with all her four months of wisdom, spoke slowly but positively. "It will be OK, Yogie, Nellie, and Boo-Boo. No need for any one of us to be afraid. You saw how nice the people that adopted our sisters were, didn't you? Karen and Winston would not allow bad people to take us away from them."

"But, Marbles, I don't want to lose you. You're the one that takes care of me. And Nellie and Boo-Boo, too. I don't want to be taken away or have any of you taken from me. We have already lost our mom and two sisters." Yogie began breathing faster and faster.

"If I am to believe what I have heard before the ringing of the doorbell, we shall all be adopted together. But it remains to be seen. I can only hope that remains true."

"It will be OK sisters," Ted-D stated. "I know my momma and daddy will not split a family up. They plan on keeping you all together, as it should be."

Nellie and Boo-Boo sat in wonderment at Ted-D's words.

"You hear us, Ted-D?" the girls asked in unison.

"Why, of course I hear you. But we can't let the humans know this. That's why, for now, we only talk telepathically."

"OK, but isn't that dishonest?" asked Nellie.

"No. Simply the way of the world. It keeps things in balance somehow," Ted-D paused. Taking a deep breath, he continued on, "OK, I really don't know why, but it has been inbred in me somehow to pass on to others such as you, my new sisters." Ted-D smiled.

Boo-Boo stated, "I hope we are your 'new' sisters. We're only four months old." Boo-Boo held up her back foot so Ted-D could count her toes.

"I see that. And very smart, too," Ted-D added. Boo-Boo smiled proudly.

Yogie cuddled in closer to her protector. "Oh, let it be true, Marbles. We can stay together as a family of four. Let it be true." Don's hand came in under the chair and took Yogie up in it. Yogie looked back at her sisters and Ted-D. Scared. Wide-eyed and scared. Marbles yelled up to her, "It will be OK, Yogie. We are here for you." Nellie and Boo-Boo nodded in acknowledgment. Still, Yogie was frightened until . . .

Don's voice was soothing. His large hand was gentle as it cupped Yogie's little body in it. Yogie began to relax; her breathing went back to normal.

"Did you hear that, Love? The multi-colored kitty meowed when I picked up her sister. It's almost like she is letting her know there is nothing to fear."

"Yes, I did. I suppose they all take care of each other since it is just them. No Momma or Daddy to take care of them. I mean, kitty parents." Gloria smiled at Karen. "I am sure you've taken great care of them all."

"Oh yes. They are family to us until we find them a good home." Karen wiped her eye. "It's always hard to let them go. Even after so many years of being foster parents to kitties, it still pulls at the heartstrings." Looking at her husband, she exclaimed, "But we are happy when a good home is found. Then we know we've done well. Don't we Winston?"

"That we do, Karen, that we do." Winston caught a kitty scampering out from under the table, scratching it behind its ear. "Sometimes we find ourselves on the verge of calling the adoptive parents-to-be and telling them we decided to keep the kittens ourselves." He smiled.

"Then we think how difficult it would be once winter arrives to travel south with these little ones." Karen interjected.

"Yes, we couldn't do that to them. Just up and leave every winter for the warmer temps. Unlike us, they would be wondering what the heck was going on."

"And that is why today we get to meet you and bid these little ones a happy farewell. But it is never easy. I guess the older one gets, the cuter these kittens get, too."

By this time, Don found himself sitting cross-legged on the floor, Yogie crawling over his legs. Nellie came over to see what this new guy was all about as Marbles sat back and watched the doings. She seemed content herself, especially after how Yogie had worried when the doorbell rang. The fourth kitten? Boo-Boo? Karen was just receiving her from Winston to give to Gloria who was already in kitten paradise, having not been around so many kittens at the same time in many years.

Taking Boo-Boo in her hands, Gloria melted, as did Boo-Boo. Curling up in a little ball of cuteness, Boo-Boo delighted in all the attention she was basking in at the moment. Paws up in the air, her head curled upside down and purring. Gloria had a sparkle in her eyes and an "ooooohhhhh" escaped her lips. Don knew then that the four girls were now going home with them.

An hour and fifteen minutes later found the kitties safely tucked in their travel cases and Don and Gloria packing the truck with so many playthings and foods for the girls that they were overwhelmed.

"Are you sure we can't give you something for all of this? I mean, we really appreciate it and the girls will, too, I am sure, but it cost so much to buy this stuff."

"Now, now, Don. Don't worry about the cost," Winston said, his hand waving away the idea of taking cash for something that he and his wife were pleased to give. "We know how much the girls enjoy these items. And the food? Well, they devour it like hungry lions. Roooaaaaarrrrr. We couldn't take a dime for any of it." Winston chuckled.

"We are just happy that the girls get to stay together as a family of four. That warms our hearts." Karen said putting an arm around Winston. "Now, Gloria, you make sure you email us on how they do, won't you?"

"Don't worry, we will send you pictures and cards at Christmas." Gloria took Don's hand in hers and squeezed it lightly. "They have found their forever home. We can't believe how lucky we are to have them to love." Gloria beamed. "We can't thank you enough for caring for them as you have."

"It is our pleasure," Winston said. "Now, Ted-D, you make sure they are well taken care of, OK?"

"I will, Sir." And with that, Ted-D put his paw out and shook Winston's hand. "Alec taught me how to be a great brother."

"And a very well-mannered one at that." Winston smiled as Ted-D seemed to glow in admiration of the words Winston spoke.

"Thank you." And with a teddy bear hug for Winston and Karen the seven of us headed towards home, the four kitties yet to be named, safely in their carriers, with Ted-D keeping a mindful eye on each.

Heading down the road with the kittens in their travel cases and Ted-D buckled in the back, Don and Gloria shared their feelings about the exceptionally caring Karen and Winston.

"What is so wow is that the adoption agency for the girls didn't charge us the usual cost. Even after they made sure the girls were all taken care of with shots and spaying." Gloria said, as she had been the one that found the girls online and dealt with the pet place that made sure the girls had a good foster home and that their needs were taken care of.

"Then you add in the cost of all the toys and food they gave us," Don added to the conversation, "it's simply beyond belief."

"I know. Wonderful people. Wonderful, caring people." Gloria answered. She peered over her shoulder to check in on Ted-D and his sisters. "Everything going well back there, Ted-D?"

"Yes, Momma. We're all doing well. Not one car sickness to report." Ted-D replied.

"Well, that is good to hear, Ted-D. We've got a long drive ahead of us so make sure you get your rest. We'll all need to be energized when we get home. Make sure you let your sisters get their rest, too."

"I will, Momma. I will." Ted-D blew Momma a kiss. Momma caught it with a smile, then returned a kiss and smile to Ted-D.

Daddy quietly drove the truck back to their home-20, with a yawn, Momma leaned back in her seat and since Ted-D and the kittens could talk without Don and Gloria knowing, Ted-D and the kittens visited until, one-by-one, each fell asleep.

***

MEW 2

As Don put the truck into park and all became quiet, Ted-D woke his sisters up with such gusto, that he even got Momma to wake up.

"Sisters! Sisters! We're home." Ted-D jumping up and down in his excitement, hit his head on the back of Don's seat.

"You OK, Ted-D?" Momma asked as she investigated the back seat area where Ted-D and his sisters were.

"Yes, Momma. I'm too excited to hurt now." Ted-D smiled.

Slowly opening their eyes, the kittens began to stretch and yawn, slowly noticing they were in the driveway of their new home.

"Wake up, Sisters, wake up," Ted-D called to them through the grates on their travel cases.

Marbles pawed the sleep from her eyes and began to look around as Yogie kept close to her side. From the other travel case, Nellie and Boo-Boo started to fidget, getting excited to see their new home.

"You're going to love your new home. I spend most of my time inside, so you'll not be alone too much. Oh, I am so glad you're my sisters."

"Ted-D," Momma called out, "wake your sisters up, we're home."

"I'm already on it, Momma. They're awake and curious as, well, as a cat. Four kitties to be exact." Ted-D laughed at his own joke.

Daddy got out of the truck and opened the back door to Ted-D and the kittens.

"Should we each take a travel case?" he asked Momma. Momma nodded her head in agreement as she went first to unlock the door. "OK, I'll take the one that Ted-D is sitting on, and you can get the other."

"Look, Momma," yelled Ted-D, "I'm riding a bucking bronco." Ted-D held his paw over his head as he sat on the travel case with Marbles and Yogie staring up at his butt.

"I see that Ted-D. Hang on tight or your sisters will buck you off."

"I will, Momma," Ted-D answered with a giggle and a "Yee Haw!"

"Shouldn't that be a 'Meow'?"

Laughing, Ted-D replied, "I suppose you are correct, Daddy. Meow! And away to the house we go."

Once inside, Momma, Ted-D, and Daddy took the kittens to their new room. In here they had already placed a bowl of water along with four bowls of food, one for each so they felt special, which they were of course. In an open used-to-be closet, there was a well-placed litter box, too.

Opening the travel cases, Momma and Daddy stood back to watch what the kitties would do. Ted-D, meanwhile, coaxed them out with words only he and the kittens could hear. (And a few Momma and Daddy could hear.)

"It's OK. See," Ted-D did a little dance in the room, "it's safe, even outside the travel cases."

Marbles, being the eldest of the four, and the biggest, took the first step into their new world. Looking around, then up at her new momma and daddy, back at Ted-D, then around the room once more, she then looked back at her sisters and said, "It's OK to come out. All is safe." Looking then at Ted-D, Marbles continued, "Since everything is new, I need to check things out, but I wish you to know, we already trust you. We can hear the caring bear in you, Ted-D, and we like that."

"I am so glad you trust me, but I'm only Ted-D, big brother of four beautiful sisters, and I do care. But I'm nooooo Care Bear. Only Ted-D."

"Oh, look," Momma said to Daddy. "It looks like Ted-D just told them a joke. Look at their faces, they all seem to be laughing."

Daddy agreed at Momma's statement, as it did look as if Ted-D had told a whopper of a joke. "He does have special skills, doesn't he?"

"Yes, he does. We are so lucky to be his parents. And the kitties' parents, too."

"Yes, we are. But now, what about their names, Love? Have you given anymore thought to that since meeting them?"

"Some thought."

"Oh, good!" Ted-D exclaimed. "I'm really curious as to what you and Momma are going to name my new sisters." Ted-D winked at his sisters and smiled.

"Ted-D, don't you want to name at least one, too?" Momma asked.

"Nope. I trust you and Daddy will name them properly."

"Well, I sure hope we don't disappoint you, or your sisters."

"I'm not worried, Momma, and neither are my sisters. I just know everything will be perfect."

Daddy looked at Momma and said, "OK. You first, what do you think their names should be?"

"No, no. You first, Honey. You first."

"Well, OK. This one here," Don began as he took a kitty off the scratching tower, "this one I would like to name Boo-Boo."

"Isn't that the one that I was holding on to at their foster parents?"

"Yes, she is. Isn't she just a little Boo-Boo? So tiny and cute." Don purred right along with Boo-Boo.

"She is indeed. Boo-Boo is her name now."

Boo-Boo smiled her cute little kitty smile and purred some more.

"OK," Don stated. "Now it is your turn to name one."

"Alrighty then," Gloria giggled. "this is fun. OK, the multi-colored one, I think she looks like a marble with all her beautiful colors, so I wish to name her Marbles." Gloria smiled awaiting Don's reaction.

"Yes, she does have beautiful colors, and like a marble, too. Marbles it is then. Hello, Marbles." Marbles looked up at Don and Gloria, and as if in approval, rolled on her back and brushed up against Gloria's foot.

"I think she likes her name. I am so glad."

"And a very good name for her, My Love."

"OK, your turn Honey."

"Well, I think I have a name for the other blond, so how about you name the grey kitty. That is, if that's OK with you."

"Oh, I was hoping I could. I've got the perfect name picked out for her too. Nellie."

"Nellie?" Don asked. "Not that it's bad, but where did that come from?" Don was smiling.

"Remember that girl on Little House on the Prairie? The one that would get in trouble at times. Well, this kitty here seems to want to explore and I can see her getting into some trouble."

"Oh, really? I only see her as being fascinated by her new home." Don smiled as Nellie clawed her way up the scratching post to be by her other sister. Eye-to-eye with Don now, Nellie stopped and looked Don right in the eye. "I believe she's an angel."

The kitty, now known as Nellie, purred and then settled in with her sister at the top of the scratching post.

"Well, time will tell. But for the moment she will be known as Nellie."

"Alright by me. Nellie can be a good kitties' name, too. You'll see." Don joked.

"OK, last kitty is yours, Honey. What are you going to name her?"

"I am thinking of naming her Midas."

"Midas? That sounds a bit strange to me. Why Midas?"

"Since there are two blondes, and this one is the darker of the two, like gold, I am sure she will have the Midas touch."

Gloria laughed as Ted-D stared at his daddy. "What?" asked Don.

"Oh, nothing. But it is different."

"And Nellie isn't?"

"Nellie fits her, Midas I'm not so sure about."

"Me neither Daddy. Are you positive?" Ted-D asked from his scratching post perch alongside Yogie, the kitty now known as Midas.

"Well, we can try it out on her for a while and see how it fits. Is that OK with you two?"

Gloria looked at Ted-D, Ted-D looked at Momma, and together, they looked at Daddy. "We suppose," they said in unison.

Ted-D gently herded all four kittens towards the alcove where the litter box was placed. "Let us show Daddy that you know where to go when you need to go pee-pee and poopy."

As each took a turn sniffing their new bathroom amenity, one of the kittens jumped in and proceeded to use it, no qualm about all of us there.

"See Daddy, my sisters know where to go potty. Momma, did you see, too?"

"Yes, I did." Gloria said. "You are teaching them so well."

"I'm glad they are quick learners, too."

"So am I, Ted-D," Daddy said with a smile.

"Sisters, did you see the new food bowls and the water bowl, too?" Ted-D simply couldn't keep his excitement contained. He wanted to show them everything at once. It brought back memories of making new friends when I was young. Still, I interrupted Ted-D.

"Yes, Daddy. What is it?"

"I just want to let you know, you do not have to show them everything right now. Let them get used to one thing and then use that as a building block."

"That's a great idea, Daddy. That way they won't get all messed up."

Don and Gloria walked out of the room to give the kitties some time to adjust, Ted-D staying behind to help them when/if needed.

So, with that, the kitties were named but not all were happy. Yogie left Ted-D's side and scrambled for the sanctity of Marbles who had now lingered over to the food bowls.

"Oh Marbles. They named me all wrong. Fix it. Please Marbles, fix it." Yogie pushed herself against Marbles side.

Marbles swallowed a bite of food and turned towards the scratching post. "Walk with me, Yogie" to which Yogie obliged.

Reaching the post, Marbles took her nails and dug into the carpet a few times. "Join me, Yogie. Scratch along for a bit with me while I explain something to you."

Yogie extended her claws into the scratching post and began going between left and right. It felt good. As she did so, Marbles began to talk.

"Yogie, my dear sister. Your sisters and I, along with Ted-D and yourself, know that our new Mom and Dad have given you a wrong name in error. They do not know what your name is yet. They need to feel it in their surroundings. Give it some time and they will learn that your name is not Midas, but Yogie."

"How do you know that?" asked Yogie as she removed a piece of carpeting from a nail.

"All of us are born with a skill or two of some sorts. This must be my skill. I cannot explain everything, but I will attempt to find answers when needed." Marbles gave Yogie a lick behind her ear.

"I don't think all living things are born with a skill." It was Nellie that said this.

"Why do you say that?" asked Marbles.

"Well, remember Mikey? That dog next door to Karen and Winston? All he seemed to do was make noise but for no positive outcome. Just to make noise."

"That is true. Mikey was a, let us just say, a creature of an unknown breed. Yet, we should give him the benefit of the doubt."

"How so, Marbles?"

"Well, Nellie, maybe his skill was to keep mosquitos away?"

"He would have done better had he been a stream then. Moving water keeps mosquitoes from having their eggs hatched. With Mikey around, we're going to have to think of thousands of names for these mosquitoes. Thanks, Mikey."

"Now, now, Nellie. Be nice."

Nellie walked over to the litter box. "Mikey should have been a tree. At least dogs could have had a place to pee." She then put her paw in her mouth, faced into the litter box, and made a gagging sound. "Mikey..."

"We have a Mikey. But we don't talk about him." It was Ted-D who was standing in the doorway to the kitties' room.

"Sometimes it is better not to talk about some stuff." Marbles said, concluding the conversation. Ted-D nodded.

Boo-Boo rolled on her back, squirming, and smiling, saying to anyone who could hear her, "Look at me, I'm Boo-Boo and I'm cute!"

***

MEW 3

Ted-D looked toward the door of the girl's room and sniffed the air.

"What do you smell, Ted-D", asked Marbles and then Marble's herself began to sniff.

"Yes, I believe it is dinner time for my sisters." Ted-D jumped down to the floor from his perch on the tower-of-power. "Follow me sisters." With that Ted-D began walking in the direction of the kitchen, waving over his head for his sisters to follow him. They did, timidly, but followed they did.

At the kitchen table sat their new daddy while new momma was at the counter opening cans of kitty food. Marbles rushed over by Gloria and began rubbing her leg in appreciation. Gloria looked down, smiling. "Are we hungry kitties?"

They looked up at her and mewed, pacing back and forth in circles. Daddy watched, enjoying the antics.

"It has been a week since we had brought them home, but I think they have already gained a few pounds." Daddy quipped.

"Oh, you hush now. They're growing kitties and they have maybe gained a pound, if that." Momma replied.

"I do know that Marble's seems to always be the first one out here and she's the biggest of her sisters."

"Maybe she has the best nose?" Momma stated.

"Could be," Daddy agreed. "I must say though, being the biggest of them all I believe she will grow into her body."

Marbles was soon joined by her sisters in interweaving themselves around Gloria's legs.

"Now, now girls, don't trip me. I'm almost ready to bring your food to your room."

All the kitties looked up with "Mew" on their lips. Or more so, "Mew, mew."

"They act like they haven't eaten in weeks," Don shared.

"They do like their food, don't they Momma?"

"Yes, they do, Ted-D. Yes, they do."

"OK, girls, time for the food train." With that, Momma waitress led the kittens to their room to devour today's dinner. Don and Ted-D followed the parade of kittens like a pair of cabooses dueting "chug, chug, chug."

"Now, now you two," Momma said over her shoulder, "only engines make noises."

"Well, today, cabooses do, too," Daddy replied to which Ted-D said, "Choo-choo." The two of them laughed.

Once the bowls were placed upon the floor, the human servants and Ted-D stood back to admire the kitties as they enjoyed their dinner. As they did so, Daddy noted, "You know, you two," he stated looking at Momma and Ted-D, "maybe you were both correct when you said you weren't sure about Midas being a good name for the other blonde."

Momma and Ted-D looked at Daddy who continued talking, "What do you two think if we named Midas, well, Yogie instead?" Yogie's head came out of the food bowl with a quick upwards look towards Daddy as Momma breathed a sigh of relief.

"That would be great. What do you think Ted-D?"

"I believe Midas would be very happy with that name." Ted-D looked at Midas, now Yogie, who had a great big smile on her face.

"As I stated before, keep in mind, we need to stay with their names as of now because they will get confused if we call them by a different name. Agreed?"

Daddy looked at Yogie, then back at Momma. "Agreed."

With that, Momma and Daddy left the room to get on with their day, leaving Ted-D and the kitties to themselves.

"Marbles," Yogie yelled over to her sister. "Marbles, did you hear that? I am now YOGIE!!!" Yogie rubbed against Marbles in pure happiness.

"Yes, I did hear that. Great news indeed."

"It is, isn't it? I was so worried that I would never get my name back. It has been a long time since I've been called by my proper name, hasn't it?"

"Yes, it has been quite some time. This is good news. Good news indeed."

With that, with full bellies and proper names, each found a spot to take a nap. Ted-D, too.

***

MEW 4

Ted-D woke up from his nap, not from enough sleep, but because of a lot of movement by Nellie who Ted-D was cuddled up with.

Gurgle, gurgle. Gurgle, gurgle. Nellie's tummy was sounding like a boiling pot of water, and it seemed like it was about to boil over.

Ted-D sat straight up as Nellie stretched her legs and opened her eyes. "Sorry about this, Ted-D. Apparently I ate a wee bit too much." With that, Nellie walked over to the litter box and began scraping a little pit in the corner, turned a few times and, facing the wall with Ted-D seeing her back end, let dinner go.

"Ewe! That's messy," noted Ted-D. "I'm glad I don't poop."

"You don't?" asked Nellie scratching the litter over the steaming pile. "I've never noticed. That can't be good at all."

"It's OK," Ted-D answered. Smiling a broad smile, he continued, "I smell foods. And it's a good thing as my stuffings would really be a mess if I ate."

"I suppose that would be nasty; I'd be saying ewe then." Nellie laughed.

Jumping out of the litter box, in attempts to get the litter out between her toes, Nellie wiped her paws on the mat. "I must admit, Ted-D, to me, this is the worst thing, litter in between my toes. Yuck!"

"Is there anything you'd like to do, Nellie? I'm not used to having anyone around this much. Usually, I just watch out the window and wait for Momma and Daddy to come home from work."

"Well, big brother Ted-D," began Nellie with a giggle out of Ted-D, "there is a blue mouse I had spied out there in the kitchen that looks like it would be fun to play with. Would you mind keeping me company with that?"

"Oh, not at all. That would be fun." And with that, Nellie sashayed and Ted-D wiggled his butt as they walked out of the kitties' room and down the hall to the kitchen.

"Now, where did that blue mouse go? I had thought I saw him under that chair over there. Don't tell me he's real," Nellie exclaimed.

"Over there, by the fridge. Maybe when Momma and Daddy went to work one of them accidently kicked him from under that chair."

"Oh, he does look like fun." Nellie went over and, with a single nail point, swiped the blue mouse up and over her head. As the blue mouse came down, Nellie rolled onto her back, tapped it with her tail in Ted-D's direction and the game of "Blue Mouse" was on.

Along about ten minutes later, time found Nellie lying under the same chair that blue mouse had been originally and before her and Ted-D began playing. Ted-D was propped against Nellie's side, his head ebbing as if sea foam on a wave. Having tuckered themselves out but were very happy, they enjoyed the time together.

"That was fun," Ted-D finally said.

"Yes, it was great fun, indeed. Thank you, Ted-D."

"No need to thank me, Nellie. I should be thanking you. If you and your sisters were not adopted by my parents, now your parents, too, I would be all alone today instead of having fun with you."

"What would you be doing?"

"Well, most of the day I would look out the front window."

"That is always fun," Nellie interjected. "Tell me, what would you see?"

"Depending on the day, I mean, if it were garbage day, I'd watch the big garbage truck go up and down the street picking up everyone's garbage. The truck would grab ahold of the garbage bins and with its big grabber, take the garbage bin to the top of the truck and shake it so all the garbage would fall into the back of the truck. Then he would go to the next house and do it all over again.

Some days the street cleaner would drive by and sweep the roadsides of all the leaves, dirt, and litter. Most days though, I would wait for mailman Bob or mailwoman Kim to deliver the mail. I like that the best because they would wave to me, and I'd wave back. They are very nice."

"That's nice when humans can understand us," Nellie agreed. "I mean, we are all in this world together. It just makes it so much easier when we all get along. No matter what our skin color, or in the case of Marbles, skin colors. If we are two-legged, or four-legged. It really shouldn't matter."

Ted-D added, "Feline or teddy bear."

"Exactly. I know I can't wait for my new mom and dad to be able to understand us. I must say though, they are doing quite well in taking care of all of us."

"They are full of love. Except for Daddy in the morning, he's like a bear, and not a teddy bear. He growls and spits like a grizzly."

"Really?" asked Nellie, eyes as big as milk saucers.

Amongst laughing spurts Ted-D answered, "Not really. But he does take a while to warm up to the day. He doesn't get mean or anything, he just doesn't like to talk when he first gets up, but later, oh my!"

"He talks a lot?"

"Oh yes!" Ted-D replied. "Like a steam engine going downhill." The two of them laughed at this bit of picturesque imagination.

With that, Ted-D laid his head back down onto Nellie's side and Nellie curled around Ted-D, almost as if Ted-D were in a cocoon. A nice, warm, purring . . .

"What's wrong, Ted-D?" Marbles asked, as she, Boo-Boo and Yogie walked into the kitchen.

Ted-D apologized, "I'm sorry. I was feeling so good wrapped up in Nellie's warmth, but then I felt the vibrations of her purrs and it reminded me of my big sister, Alec."

Marbles tapped Nellie on the head. "Wake up Nellie. Ted-D is feeling sad and needs us now."

"What? Where am I?" Nellie looked around. "Oh, yes. OK. What did you say Marbles?" Nellie yawned, stretching her body from head to toe.

"Ted-D is feeling sad, and we should all try to understand why he is feeling that way. Maybe we can help our new brother feel better. Now, what is wrong Ted-D?"

Ted-D sat up with a sniffle, moving his paws like airplane propellers to dry his eyes before his stuffings got wet. "I miss my sister." Ted-D's eyes welled up once again.

Marbles nodded, "That is understandable. It hasn't been that long since Alec went over the Rainbow Bridge, has it?"

"No, only about eighty-one days. I lost track after fifty days."

"You have been counting the days?"

"Yes. I thought once I counted one hundred days that I wouldn't miss her anymore."

Marbles sat down near Ted-D and put an arm around him the best she could.

"That's a nice thought, but do you want to forget your big sister?"

Ted-D looked at Marbles as Yogie and Boo-Boo came closer. "No, I don't ever want to really forget my big sister. But I don't want to have the pain anymore."

"Well, Ted-D, I hate to tell you this, but the pain is always going to be there. Maybe not as big and hurting as it is now, but there will always be that part inside that hurts."

Ted-D looked at Marbles with deep sorrow in his eyes. "But why? I don't like this pain. It hurts."

"Why? Because you were lucky enough in your life to have had a big sister so nice as Alec. I mean, she must have been very special to you if you are hurting this much."

"Yes, she was." Ted-D sniffed.

"And that is why the pain is so big. Many individuals will never experience that kind of hurt because they will never know someone as special as Alec."

"So, I should feel good that I hurt so bad?"

"In a roundabout way, yes."

"That sucks," as soon as the words left Ted-D's mouth, he caught himself, "Oops. Sorry. That was bad to say."

All four kittens laughed. "That's OK, Ted-D, we won't tell Momma and Daddy. And you know, you are right, it sucks. But count your blessings that you knew Alec. A priceless part of your life."

"Thanks, Marbles." Ted-D gave her a hug and then Boo-Boo, jumping up and down, gleefully shouted, "Group hug, group hug."

Ted-D and his sisters were bathed in the warmth of love, and at that moment, a new sister and brotherhood arrived. A bond was formed, and a new family unit was born.

***

MEW 5

Don walked into the kitties' room. Seeing Yogie sitting on the desk, looking out the window, he picked her up and cradled her in his arms. She purred.

"You are the world's best purrer, you know that, Yogie?" She smiled up at him and purred even more. He rubbed her belly as she did so.

"So soft, my buddy, so soft." He gave her a hug. "Oh, so that is what caught your attention," Don said, seeing the snowflakes outside the window. "Oh, my. And this is your first snow. What do you think of it?"

Yogie looked out the window, then back up to Don's eyes and purred again.

"I am going to think that means you like it." He laughed. "Here, let me put you down and bring some inside for you."

Yogie jumped from Don's hands and went to the top of the tower-of-power in her room and waited. She did not know what to expect but she was excited.

Don opened the door to the backyard and knelt. Taking a handful of the white, fluffy flakes into his hands, he arose, stepped inside, and closed the door behind him.

Slowly putting the snowball near Yogie, he asked what she thought of it, almost as if she could tell him in words he would understand. But he asked anyway. Her expression was priceless.

Yogie put her nose near the snowball and sniffed. It didn't seem to smell like anything other than water with a bit of something, of what she was not sure. She then took her paw and slowly reached out and touched this mysterious, white, cold, ball.

"Ooooo, that is cold," she said out loud, to which Don only heard, "Meow."

She watched in amazement as the snowball began to melt.

"Pretty cool, huh, Yogie?"

Yogie again looked up at Don and purred.

"I'll take the rest of this into the bathroom and put it in the sink, otherwise it is going to make a mess in here."

As Don entered the bathroom, he spied Ted-D sitting there on the sink, swinging his legs back and forth.

"I heard you brought snow in the house. Can I smell it?"

"Why, of course you can."

Ted-D began sniffing at the ball of white stuff, sparkles in his eyes.

"First snow is always the best snow to smell, Daddy. After that, one never knows what you may find in it."

"That is true Ted-D, one never knows."

"And if it looks yellow, don't go near it. Once it gets into your paws, it sticks with you for some time. Yuck!"

"Yuck!" Daddy echoed back.

As soon as Don released the snowball into the sink, Yogie's sisters arrived and jumped up on the sink counter to see what the fuss was all about. Each taking a sniff and a wee bit of a swat with their paws, examining this new toy. Below them, Yogie was getting ready to jump up to join them in their learning.

"A special occasion for all of you girls. This is snow. Cold, wet, snow. A fun thing the first few times, but then after that, at least for me, it gets old. Snow removal is not that much fun. What is fun, though, is enjoying watching all of you seeing it for the first time." Don smiled, he felt like a Daddy again, even though it was to kitty cats. He didn't mind. They were little and new to the world. He would help guide the best he knew. He was beginning to get attached.

Don left the girls to their curiosity and went to his office to work on music and writing tasks. Eventually the girls, who the kitties were getting to be known as, sauntered off to take their nap. All except one. Nellie.

"Mew."

Don was busy at the desk, working on something important to him.

"Mew."

It was faint, but Don heard it this time. Looking over the right arm of the chair he was sitting in, he sees Nellie looking back up at him.

"Mew."

"Oh, buddy, this is a nice surprise. Come here." Don rotated the chair to face Nellie and picked her up, hugging her to his chest. "How are you doing? Are you keeping watch while your sisters sleep?" Don then took Nellie into both his hands and gently held her arm's-length from his body.

There was a deep, soulful look in her eyes. Don smiled. So did Gloria who was standing in the doorway to the office.

"She seems to be attracted to you, Honey."

"What do you mean," Don scoffed, enveloping Nellie to his bosom once again, "she's just lonely with her sisters sleeping."

"They say that female cats are more attracted to the guys than they are to women. I'm thinking she is going to have herself wrapped around your heart in no time." Gloria smiled.

"I have no idea what you mean," Don replied, giving Nellie another hug.

Ted-D appeared from behind Momma's legs. "Oh, look at Daddy. Daddy's a softy when it comes to kittens, isn't he Momma?"

"He sure is, Ted-D, he sure is." They both walked out of the office, smiling, leaving Nellie to take a nap in Don's arms.

Don woke up some time later only to find Nellie tugging at Billie, the sheepskin rug that Don had bought Alec-the-Cat a year before she crossed the Rainbow Bridge.

"Nellie," Daddy scorned her with a roughness in his voice that she was not used to hearing. "Nellie, what are you doing? You treat Billie nice or I'll have to put her away until you get older." Don raised his eyebrows looking as if he was waiting for Nellie to answer. She did indeed answer, but not as expected.

Nellie looked up at Don sitting in his chair, then with her teeth, little as they were but very sharp, began tugging at Billie once more, paws holding Billie to the floor as she did so.

"OK, that's it." Don got out of his chair and picked Billie up. "If you can't treat Billie nicely, then Billie will be put away for a while.

Billie was Alec's comforter when we were at work or had gone away. Alec could cuddle with her, and she would make her feel safe from all harm.

Now, I'm not mad at you, Nellie. I know you are learning so very much at this point in your life. So, right now, I'm just going to put Billie away until you get a little older, OK?"

Nellie looked up as if she understood. And purred.

***

MEW 6

"OK, girls," Momma yelled into the rooms away from the kitchen. "Time for supper."

That's all it took. All four came running in from where they had been, Marble's in the lead followed by Nellie, then Yogie and Boo-Boo. They all scurried around Momma, rubbing her legs and putting their paws up on the counter doors, meowing and mewing all the while.

"They sure do look tall when they stretch themselves out, standing on their hind legs like that, don't they?" Don asked from his seat at the table, enjoying the doings.

"Yes, they have grown some since we got them, haven't they?" agreed Gloria. "And take a look at how much they play and run around. They are fit for their size."

"It would be cool if they kept getting bigger though, wouldn't it?" Don said with a grin.

"Only if you want to get another job. Couldn't you imagine how much food and litter would cost if they got bigger?"

"Ooo, I did not think of that. Still, it would be cool if they did get to be the size of a mountain lion. I could take them for walks around the neighborhood, scaring the dogs while holding onto the girls chain link leashes." Don laughs as he imagines it. "Couldn't you see that, Love?"

"Not the way you are telling it, Honey. What I am seeing is you holding onto those chain link leashes as the girls drag you around the neighborhood and the dogs sitting back and howling at you as you all go by."

"Yup, you are probably correct," Don laughed. "Got me on that one, Love."

Gloria picked up the four bowls and began to head off to the girl's room. "OK, girls. It's Food Train time. Choo-Choo!"

"Yay, parade," Don chimed in. "I so do love a great parade. Oh, look at the engine. Marbles you look great, Nellie is a coal car and would you look at the other two. Which one is going to be the caboose tonight? Oh, look. Yogie is the caboose," Don stated as Boo-Boo raced ahead of her sister. "Oh my. A grand parade. A great, grand parade. I so do love a great, grand parade. Yes, I do."

"OK, Daddy. Enough is enough," Ted-D said as he came up from the basement. "My sisters are already in their room eating." Ted-D laughed.

Next thing they knew, here comes Marbles, racing back to the kitchen, followed by all her sisters.

"Well, what is going on here, Love?"

"I don't know. Well, I do know that Marbles would rather have treats first. She simply does the parade to make sure there will be food in their room before going for the treats."

"Maybe they are getting tired of their food?" Don asked.

"That is a possibility. They are getting bigger as you said. Maybe they are past kitten food already?"

"Only one way to find out."

"Yes, the next time we go shopping we'll get some different food for them to try out."

As time traversed, the train continued doing the roundabout. No, it did not matter what food they got served, Marbles always led the group back to have dessert first. Oh well. They are cats. Do you want to try and tell them differently? Nope? Me neither.

***

MEW 7

The next few weeks saw more snow appear outside the windows, less sunlight, and, since he was on shutdown at the place where he worked, more of Don. December. Brrrrr.

The girls got a bit bigger each day and began to get more acquainted with the rest of the house, from the living room to the basement. It was nice that the four sisters were together. They kept each other company and, for the most part, played nice together.

There were times that Don and Gloria would wake up in the night only to hear a bit of roughhousing, but that was about it, for now. We all know how siblings can be, so both were happy the girls got along. Ted-D was happy about that, too.

Each day being a new adventure for the girls, today would be no different, although a big surprise awaited. For whom? Only time would answer that. But it was a doozie.

Meanwhile, the girls sat in the living room watching the snowflakes come down; Ted-D right alongside them. All watching in amazement. Mother Nature was putting on quite a show. Eventually, the snow stopped, the girls and Ted-D got tired, and they all curled up together and fell asleep within the blankets on the couch.

Don was enjoying his time at home, with no people around, only kitties and Ted-D, plus, of course, Gloria. During the day she had her job to go to, and Don would work on projects around the house. This included making meals which he enjoyed.

Many years ago, when Don and Gloria began co-habiting together, it was agreed amongst the two of them, with great delight for each, that Don would do the cooking and Gloria would do the dishes. It was a good decision that each was glad they had made together.

Don found the kitchen to be sort of like an inside shop, where the pots and pans and such were the tools, the spices a bonus while Gloria could listen to her gem show whilst relaxing and keeping her hands busy in the bubbles of the sink.

Today, Don's project was organizing the basement which had multiple rooms. It was Don's hope to get at least the family room organized, the extra canning jars put into their own area, and his music room equipment set up for when he could get a chance playing the sax between projects. It was a lot on his list, but that was how he did things. Fill up your time and get it done.

A few hours later, the sun going to bed outside left no natural light in the basement area, so Don called it a day and went upstairs to grab a snack. Ted-D woke up as Don opened the refrigerator door.

"Hi, Daddy," Ted-D said from the entrance to the kitchen. He stretched his arms and yawned.

"Did you have a good nap with your sisters, Ted-D?"

"I did. But then one of them kicked me in the head with her paw and woke me up."

"Oh, that wasn't nice, Ted-D. Which one did that?"

"I don't know. I was sleeping when it happened and when I woke up, they were all sleeping, too."

"OK, at least it wasn't on purpose then."

"No, Daddy. It was in their sleep. Kind of like when Momma kicks her leg out from under the blanket." Ted-D yawned again.

"Would you like to join me for a little snack, Ted-D?"

"What are you having, Daddy?"

"Just a couple of Christmas cookies that I made and a glass of milk."

"That sounds good, Daddy."

And with that, Ted-D jumped up on Daddy's leg, crawled onto the table and sniffed at the milk and cookies because, as we all know, Ted-D only sniffs food.

As the last morsel of cookie disappeared, Don asked, "Well, Ted-D, how are you doing? One more cookie?"

"No thanks, Daddy. My sniffer is tired." Ted-D rolled onto his back, facing the window. "Geez, Daddy, the snow is all over the driveway. Do you think Momma will be able to get in?"

Don looked out the window. "Good thing you noticed that Ted-D. I better get out there and at least clear the drive for Momma. I can take care of the sidewalks when it's all done snowing tonight."

"I'll watch out the window." And with that, Ted-D scampered off to the living room window to watch Don clear the snow from the drive.

Sometime later, Don came in, stomping his boots on the mat and removing his jacket and hat. Taking his gloves, he brushed the snow off his pant legs.

"You did great, Daddy. Now Momma can get inside where its warm." Ted-D smiled a big smile.

Behind Ted-D, there came a flurry of kitty sisters. Looking at Don's boots, they exclaimed in unison, "Mew!" and came forth to check out the snow which was already melting off the boots.

Donning his slippers, Don went into the kitchen and made himself a cup of coffee then proceeded to the living room. Once in his chair, he reclined back, putting a blanket on him that Kayla Kitten, Ted-D's human sister, had made. A nice, heavy blanket that he himself liked to cuddle up in.

It was not long afterwards that Ted-D came bounding in, his sisters trailing close behind, and like a circus act, they all jumped on Don and burrowed within the folds of the blanket. Don indeed felt loved.

"Daddy," Ted-D looked up at Don from within the cozy blanket. "Daddy?"

"Yes, Ted-D." Don sipped at his coffee.

"Can you tell us a story?"

"A story? What kind of a story?"

"A happy story. The story about the day we first met my sisters." Ted-D smiled at Yogie, Boo-Boo, Nellie, and Marbles. "That is a happy story, isn't it, Daddy?"

"One of the happiest stories I know, Ted-D. OK. I can do that." With that, Ted-D lay back with his arms behind his head, legs crossed, yet under the blanket and cuddled with his sisters as Don cleared his throat and began telling them the story of how they all first met.

.
.
.
.
.
.

Taking a sip of his coffee, and watching the girls begin to stir a bit, Don finished the story. . . "As time went on, names were decided on with only one change...

Boo-Boo, Yogie, Marbles, and Nellie have a fondness for water when it comes out of a faucet. They enjoy laying in sinks and bathtubs and chasing each other around the house. They love their mouse toys and blue twirlers. They took over Alec-the-Cat's towers-of-power and they love Ted-D like they love catnip. But I suppose you all know that. Don't you?"

Don looked down at the kitties in his lap. Yes, all four of them. And smiled.

Outside the window, the sound of a vehicle pulling into the driveway got the girls a bit excited and found Ted-D bounding for the window, jumping onto the back of the couch.

Looking back at his sisters and Daddy, Ted-D exclaimed, "Momma's home. Momma's home."

"Did you hear that, girls? Ted-D sees Momma pulling into the driveway. Time to get up now."

Boo-Boo looked up at Don, extended her legs out, yawned, smiled, and said … "Mew. Momma's home".

***

MEW 8

Don looked down at Boo-Boo and asked in surprise, "Did I just hear you talk, Boo-Boo?"

"Well, that took long enough." It was Marbles making this statement.

Don looked over at Marbles in astonishment. "You talk, too?"

"Of course," Nellie got involved now. "We all talk. We're cats, are we not?"

Don replied, "I thought it was just a gift that Alec had."

"Alec was a cat. We are cats. Cats talk. People simply need to listen to the world around them. So many things to enjoy. We are only a small part."

"You must be the wise kitty?" Don inquired of Marbles.

"That is what I have been told." Marbles answered.

A voice from the floor rose up. "I'm Boo-Boo, the cute one."

"And so you are." Don smiled.

"My twin of the same color is the quiet one." Boo-Boo explained Yogie's quiet nature. "But she is cute, too." Boo-Boo rolled head over tail onto her back, legs up in the air like a puppy.

"Well, that was different," remarked Don.

Boo-Boo looked up from the floor. "I'm Boo-Boo and I'm cute. Rub my tummy? Please?"

Don couldn't help but smile as he bent down to rub Boo-Boo's belly. As he did so, Ted-D suddenly jumped off the couch and raced toward the kitchen. That was when the rest of them heard the kitchen door opening. Momma was home.

"Boy, is your mother going to be surprised." Don got up and, with a bit of excitement in his step, followed them into the kitchen.

Ted-D was the first to greet Momma when she got in the door, followed by his sisters and finally Daddy.

Giving Gloria a kiss, Don said, "You are not going to believe this, Love."

"What's that," she asked as she hung up her coat.

Gloria looked down to see all four kitties sitting on the kitchen floor with Ted-D in the middle of them, looking up at her, like a chorus in sync, they said, "Hi, Momma." Gloria glowed.

"Awwww, I have been waiting so long for this moment." She knelt down and hugged them all, Ted-D included of course.

"You've been waiting for this moment?" Don asked, puzzled.

"Yes, it was driving me crazy. Each kitty is different, as some may not talk for a year or more."

"Why didn't I know this?" Don asked, a hurt look on his face as if he had missed out on something huge.

"That could be because you are doing more talking than listening. I told you all kitties talk."

"You did?"

"Yes, when you first heard Alec talking, I explained it then."

"Really?"

By now, the girls and Ted-D were getting motion sickness moving their heads back and forth between Momma and Daddy.

"Yes, I did. I'm pretty sure that I did. Either way, all kitties talk."

"That is so cool!" By now, Don had joined Gloria by kneeling on the floor, petting the kitties, and rubbing Ted-D's shoulder. "This is so cool," Don repeated.

Smiling, nodding her head in the affirmative, Gloria agreed, "Yes, it is." Inside her being, Gloria beamed.

(See, I told you there was going to be some big news coming up, didn't I? Pretty cool surprise, too, wasn't it?)

***

I've never had more than one cat at a single time before, so it was interesting to hear how each sounded when they meowed. Much more than that, it was most interesting to hear how each sounded when they talked. Now that is one thing that never happened for me, that is, the ability to hear cats talk. Well, except for Alec. I sure do miss her.

***

MEW 9

It was Wednesday night and Ted-D was getting his sisters ready for Kayla Kitten's arrival.

"Sisters. Sisters!" Ted-D was calling out and jumping up and down with excitement. "Hurry up sisters. Kayla will be here soon."

All four sisters, one behind the other, ran from their room and into the living room where Ted-D was waiting on the fireplace mantel with Little Kitty.

Yogie, Boo-Boo, Nellie, and Marbles plopped onto their butts, tails swung behind them as they did so and looked up at Ted-D.

"OK, Ted-D, what is the rush?" It was Marbles who asked the question.

"Kayla comes over every Wednesday after work to visit Momma and Daddy. After supper, Momma and Kayla come into the living room here to watch Jeopardy. That's when we begin to have fun."

"We?" asked Nellie.

"Yes, we. Me and Little Kitty and now all of you, my sisters. That is, if you want to join us. It's fun."

"Well, before we talk about what it is that you do with this Kayla - or is it, Kayla Kitten? – who is this Little Kitty next to you on the mantel?" It was Marbles once again who asked the question.

"Oh. Little Kitty is my sister that Momma lets me play with. She got Little Kitty from Uncle Wayne a long time ago. I know she's not real, but like a stuffed animal would be to humans. She's my, I guess, stuffed animal." Ted-D laughed. "But I believe her to be real."

"Nothing wrong with that," Marbles replied. "Now, what is it that you and Little Kitty do with this Kayla," Marbles cleared her throat, "or Kayla Kitten?"

"Her name is Kayla, but Daddy calls her Kayla Kitten. That's because Momma always liked cats, so he started calling Momma, Momma Cat and Kayla, Kayla Kitten. And what Little Kitty and I do with Kayla is stare at her from the fireplace mantle. It's like we bond with Kayla then. And won't she be surprised if my sisters would join in the staring, bonding ritual?"

"Well, that does sound like a nice time and all, but would it be OK if we would jump on her and get her to give us belly rubs?" asked Boo-Boo. "I like belly rubs."

"I suppose that would be OK," Ted-D replied. "I mean, we would all be together with Momma and Kayla and that's what is important. Time spent together."

"Does Daddy join in?" Nellie asked.

"No, Daddy usually has work to do. He's either in the office, or downstairs in his music room practicing music on his sax or outside working on something."

"He is busy, isn't he?"

"Yes, he is, Nellie. He states he wants to get everything ready for retirement and before his body doesn't move like it does now."

"Ted-D is that Kayla coming up to the house now?" asked Yogie.

"Yay! Yes, it is." And with that Ted-D got on his belly, wrapping an arm around Little Kitty and began to warm up to stare. The sisters all scampered to the kitchen to wait for Kayla to enter the side door.

With a smooth motion, the door opened up and there was Kayla, more precise, Kayla Kitten, black hair, a bit taller than Momma and carrying a bag of wash.

"Hi there, Kayla Kitten."

Kayla turned around as she closed the door. Looking a bit mystified, she spied the kitties near the kitchen counter looking up at her.

"Oh my. Mom did say there would be a surprise tonight. You all must be the surprise." Kayla put her laundry bag down and knelt at the step into the kitchen. The kitties made their way to her for pets and belly rubs as they were hoping to receive.

After supper, just as Ted-D had stated, Kayla and Momma went into the living room to watch Jeopardy. The kitties joined in as did Ted-D and Little Kitty. That is, all but one. Nellie.

Nellie found Daddy working at the desk in his office. Nellie walked in quietly and proceeded to sit near Don, watching him at the desk. After a bit, Don noticed Nellie in the shadow of the desk light.

"Hi there, buddy. How are you doing?"

Nellie looked up and replied, "I'm not sure." Don noticed a tear in her eye.

"Here, come on up on my lap and we can talk a bit. Would you like that?"

Nellie took a paw and dabbed at the tears, nodding in the affirmative to Don's question.

"Here, let me wrap the blanket around you. I know I like it like that, all cuddled up on a winter's night."

Nellie wrapped herself in a ball and cuddled within the folds of the blanket.

"Now, if I see correctly, you're hurting a bit inside?"

Nellie nodded. "Yes, I am. I don't want to offend you or Momma, but it is hard to call you and Momma Daddy and Momma. I mean, I like you both a lot and know you are taking care of me and my sisters, but I get scared."

"Scared?" Don asked as he petted Nellie. "About what?"

"Well, scared that my sisters and I will be given away again. Then we must get used to another place all over. It's not easy never knowing where one belongs."

"You have nothing to worry about, Nellie. You and your sisters will always have a home with us."

"We will? Are you sure?"

"Yes, I am sure. I know how you feel and I do not want you to ever worry about not having a home. You'll always be with us. You and your sisters. A family."

"Oh, that does sound nice. I never had a family I could call my own."

"Me neither. Not until your mother and I got together."

"Really? You didn't have a family?"

"Not until now."

"What about your mom and dad? Didn't they love you?"

"Well, let me say they did the best they could. But not until now do I really feel the love of a family."

"You did the same for Kayla, too, didn't you?"

"Yes, I suppose you could say that. She is part of your mother, so of course, I love her like she is my own, too. Family. We stick together."

Nellie purred as she looked up at Don. "Thank you, Daddy."

"For what?"

"For helping us become one. To be a family." Nellie got up and put her arms around Don. "To be loved."

***

MEW 10

Marble's ears perked up and like dominos, so did her sister's ears. They knew that sound and all went running to the kitchen. Food!

Scurrying around the corner in the hallway, the Indy 500 had competition that would have been hard to get in front of as the kittens made their way to the kitchen counter where Momma was putting food in their bowls.

"OK, is everyone ready?"

It was a question that did not need answering. Marbles was rubbing herself against Momma's legs as the other three meowed and purred, all the while concentrating on the food bowls Momma was just now beginning to grasp.

"OK, here we go. Choo-chooo." Off the five of them went, four four-leggers, and Momma. Going past Daddy's office, they heard Daddy clapping and shouting, "Yay, a parade. I love parades. Oh, where is the train?" he asked as Momma passed the doorway.

"Right behind me," Momma shouted over her shoulder as Marbles, Nellie, Boo-Boo, and Yogie scampered behind.

"Here we are," they all yelled at Daddy. "Choo-chooooo."

Momma went to put the food down in their dinner nook and turned around to get out of the kitties way.

"Oh my, what is this?" Momma asked.

The kitties stopped so fast that Yogie, bringing up the rear of the train collided with Boo-Boo who collided with Nellie who then collided with Marbles who was the engine of the train. They all looked up at Momma with a bit of fear in their eyes.

"Well, this is not like you girls," Momma said, returning from the bathroom with some tissue to pick up the bit of poo lying on the floor. "Who missed the litter box?"

The kitties looked at Momma, not sure what to do or say.

"It's OK. I'm just curious so we can make sure this doesn't happen again."

"It was Yogie," Boo-Boo said. "But it wasn't her fault. We were all playing and then Marbles jumped on Yogie and poo came flying out of her butt."

By then, Ted-D had walked into the girl's room to see what was going on. When he heard this, he began laughing hysterically, rolling on the floor and giggling.

"It's not funny, Ted-D," Yogie said embarrassed. "I didn't mean to do that. It just happened. It was a surprise poop."

"Of course it's not your fault," chimed in Nellie. "It's Marbles fault. She's fat. Just look at her."

Marbles eyes began to wet from tears that escaped her eye lids. "I can't help it. I like to eat. But I also like to play with my sisters, too." Now, the tears began to flow.

Ted-D stopped laughing and the room became awfully quiet. Until Daddy walked in.

"What's going on with the dining car of the train? I don't hear any eating going on."

"I don't ever want to eat again," Marbles said and ran out of the room.

"What just happened?" Daddy asked.

After hearing what all had taken place, Daddy stated he would be right back and went looking for Marbles. When he found her hiding under a blanket in one of the many boxes in the living room, he sat down in the chair closest to and asked her to come out so they could talk.

"Oh, Marbles. It does hurt, to have your sisters pick on you, doesn't it?"

Marbles looked up with heavy eyes as she cuddled into Daddy's arms and nodded.

"They weren't thinking. They just said the first thing that was on their tongue and it hurt your feelings. But let me tell you, you are not fat. One day you'll grow into your body, and you'll be the right size for you. And if you end up bigger than your sisters, so what? The main thing is that you'll be healthy and happy."

"But I still want to play. I want to have fun, too."

"Oh, Marbles. You can still have fun and play. You just need to change it up a bit since your sisters are a bit thinner than you. That's all."

"That's all? You make it sound so easy Daddy. But I'm still worried I'll hurt someone."

"I'm sure that everything will be OK. You won't hurt anyone."

"Are you sure Daddy? How do you know?"

"Well, I made the same mistake your sisters made with you. Many years ago, when I was in grade school, I had told a girl that she was fat."

"You said that, Daddy? How could you do that?"

"I wasn't thinking, just like your sisters weren't thinking. And just like your sisters, I hurt her feelings. She never talked to me after that. She just went into the school crying and never talked to me since."

"Didn't you apologize?"

"Yes, I did, but it was too late. I made her feel bad in front of the school kids and that made a lasting impression on her. I never forgave myself for that. No one should ever put another living soul down just to make themselves feel better."

"No, they shouldn't." Marbles wiped a final tear away.

Don gave Marbles a hug and then asked her if it would be OK if they all had a talk together. Marbles agreed. And after they talked, Marbles did indeed eat as she always had. And why not? She was a growing girl, just like her sisters.

***

MEW 11

"The sky is falling. I m-m-m-mean the stars are falling. Ok, I don't know what is falling from above us, but it is falling. Look." Nellie took her paw and raised it above Yogie's shaking body, pointed towards the window.

"Oh, girls, it's OK. That's snow." Daddy petted Nellie, taking turns between Yogie and Boo-Boo.

Ted-D giggled a bit, then apologized, "Sorry, sisters. I shouldn't have laughed. I mean, I didn't know what that was the first time I saw it myself."

"Snow. I thought that is what it was." Marbles sauntered in. "Nothing but snow. Nothing to be afraid of." Marbles jumped up into Daddy's lap and cleared her throat. Then, looking into Daddy's eyes, she inquired,

"We had seen snow before but nothing like this. What is happening?"

"Would you like to explain, Ted-D?"

"I can do that, Daddy. Sisters, snow is simply rain that has frozen. Instead of a rainstorm we are having a snowstorm. We have now officially left summer behind with the nice warm temperatures and will now enter Winter. The time of snow, warm blankets, and hibernation. Ahhhhh."

"So, all is, OK? The sky is not falling?" Boo-Boo asked, peeking her head from under Yogie.

"All is well. It doesn't bother us that much as it stays outside. It only bothers Momma and Daddy."

"Why does it bother them if it stays outside?" Nellie asked.

"Well, Momma and Daddy have to drive in it sometimes and Daddy has to keep the sidewalks and drive clear, so everyone is safe."

"So, we will be, OK?" Nellie asked again.

"Yes, all of us will be OK. Follow me and I'll show you how we can huddle in the blankets." Ted-D jumped from the shelf with a colump as he landed near Marbles who asked, "Would Ted-D like a ride on my back?"

With Ted-D on Marbles' back and with Nellie, Yogie, and Boo-Boo close behind, they all journeyed to the living room so as Ted-D could show his sisters the blankets that would keep them warm until spring. Together, they sang a happy song:

♫ "Hey, Ho, let it snow ♮
♯ We've all got blankets to keep us warm
Hey, Ho, let it snow ♫
♯ We're inside with our sisters and Ted-D and Momma and Daddy and . . . " ♪ ♫

No, it did not rhyme, but all of them sang in happiness and that is what matters most in these times of fearing snow, doesn't it?

***

"I don't think we will be putting up a tree anymore. I mean, we couldn't with Alec, now we certainly cannot with four kitties in the house."

"What is Momma talking about Ted-D?"

"Well, Boo-Boo, Christmas is coming and some people put trees up in their homes."

"Is that so their dogs don't have to go potty in the snow?" asked Nellie.

"No," Ted-D replied, while still laughing. "Their dogs still go out to go potty in the winter. They even take them for walks in that white stuff. But the trees Momma is talking about are called Christmas trees."

"Christmas trees?" inquired Marbles.

"Yup, Christmas trees. Some people have artificial trees and other people bring in real trees to their homes. They then decorate them in festive lights and decorations."

"And the reason they do this?" asked Marbles.

"There are many reasons. Many, many reasons. Some people do it for religious beliefs, others do it to take the winter doldrums out of their homes and replace it with merriment. What I like best is we get gifts."

"Gifts?" It was Yogie who perked her ears up to this statement.

"Yup. On Christmas morning we get up and there will be gifts under people's trees."

"But if Momma states no tree, then I shall be under the impression that we will not see a gift?"

"Not so, Marbles. Momma and Daddy still have connections to Santa Claus."

"Santa who?"

"Santa Claus. He's a big, jolly guy all dressed up in red with a big white beard. He comes along at Christmas time and gives everyone gifts."

"Seriously? You really believe that Ted-D?"

"Yes, I do Marbles. I mean, there are always gifts on Christmas morning, even for Momma, Daddy, and Kayla."

"Oh, I like that," Nellie said. "So, we might get gifts then, too?"

"Oh, yes. We all get gifts. Cool, huh?"

"Well, I don't quite understand the concept, but I am OK with it."

"Good to hear, Marbles." Nellie said. "Don't ruin a good thing."

"I was just saying I was OK with that."

"I know and I was just saying don't ruin a good thing." Nellie hissed.

"What is going on in here?" It was Daddy.

Looking up at Don Ted-D replied, "I was just explaining Christmas to my sisters."

"Ah, yes, first Christmas for your sisters. An exciting time, isn't it?"

Ted-D agreed, "Yes, it is."

Christmas morning came and with it boxes, bags, and papers that the girls enjoyed playing with. Later, as Kayla and Momma visited in the living room, Don went to the kitchen to make Christmas dinner. Nellie followed.

"Oh, Nellie, you don't have to be in here with me. Why don't you play with your sisters. Enjoy the day."

"That's OK, Daddy. I'll play with them later. I want to spend some time with you today. You always seem so busy."

"I know, but things need to get taken care of when time allows."

"Yet, you look sad, Daddy. What's wrong?"

"You do seem to be getting wiser, Nellie. You can tell, huh?"

"Yes. Talk with me Daddy. What's wrong."

"It's just that I always feel like I'm in a rush. I tend to miss out on stuff or time with those I care about and love. And then when they are gone, there is no getting that time back."

"You miss Alec, don't you, Daddy?"

"Yes, I do. Among so many others that have come and gone in my life."

"Talk to me. Tell me about the ones you miss. Let it out."

Don looked at Nellie and, sitting down at the kitchen table, left her jump on his lap and began getting his thoughts out. All while holding Nellie tight to his bosom. Nellie took it all in, looking over Don's shoulder, she listened.

***

As what happens with each day, holiday or not, Christmas came and went, gifts opened and played with, some even eaten and then it happened. Spring!

***

MEW 12

Looking out at the opened screen door, Don held onto Marbles, rubbing her ear when suddenly, the school bus going by backfired, causing Marbles to jump out of Don's arms and hide behind a chair.

"It's OK buddy. It's only a school bus."

Marbles peered out from behind the chair. "Are you sure it's, OK? It's loud and sounds scary."

"Yes, it's OK."

Marbles came out from behind the chair and returned to Don's arms. "Please don't tell anyone that I got scared of a school bus."

"Now, now, we all get scared at times. It happens to all of us."

"Even you, Daddy?"

"Even me, Marbles."

"Still, please don't tell anyone. Will you?"

"Don't worry, buddy. It's our little secret."

"Thank you. I mean, they all think I'm so tough and I would hate for them to think about me any differently. Then how would they feel when they need me to protect them?"

"I understand, Marbles. You are the caretaker of the bunch, aren't you?"

"Yes, I am. I didn't ask to be, it just happened. I really don't mind either. I feel rather important doing it."

"Well, you are important, buddy. And again, I won't tell anyone."

"Thanks, Daddy. Hey look, a squirrel."

Don turned from Marbles to look out the door in time to see the squirrel this time jump when the next school bus that went by also backfired.

"See, even that squirrel got scared. But, hey, you didn't jump this time, did you?"

"Why would I? It was only a school bus backfiring." Marbles smiled at Don. "I guess things can be scary the first time but not so much the second time."

"At times, that is true. Other times, it doesn't matter how many times, it might always scare us. Like someone sneaking up behind us and yelling boo."

"I can see that happening."

"Boo!"

Don jumped in fright. Turning around he spied on Ted-D and Nellie, rolling on the floor in laughter.

"Oh! Funny you two. Simply funny." Then Don began to laugh, too.

***

MEW 13

Walking into the girl's room, heading for the backdoor on this beautiful Saturday morning, Don noticed Marbles, Nellie, and Yogie on the desk near the window.

"What are you all up to there?" he asked.

All three turned around and, shushing Daddy, whispered for him to join them. Don quietly walked over and looked out the window.

"See the chipmunk, Daddy?" Nellie asked as her sisters each pointed a paw towards the twisted, old tree outside their window. "He's right there in that hollow spot of the tree trunk."

"Oh, I do. He's cute, huh?"

"He'd make a great toy," Nellie replied, Yogie and Marbles nodding in agreement.

"I suppose he would for you girls. Good thing for him, he's outside."

"And look over there, a bunny." Yogie pointed past the tree to where the bunny was sitting in the shade. "There is so much to watch outside this window. It's fun."

Marbles agreed, "Yes, it is."

"Well, you girls enjoy yourselves. I've got to get outside and get some things done. Where's Boo-Boo?"

"She's up on the tower-of-power."

Don looked up and over his shoulder to see Boo-Boo sleeping so cute, purring. A few steps over from where he was standing, Don reached out and began to rub Boo-Boo's belly.

Opening her eyes, she stretched a front leg toward Don, extended her nails and grasped one of his fingers, pulling him closer. She left out a long purr, then released Don's finger. Sitting up now, she began noodling the tower-of-power looking as if she were on stage singing the Blues. All in the room listened intently until Boo-Boo settled back down to go to sleep. It was beautiful, the song Boo-Boo sang. As beautiful as she was.

As Don went out to the yard, the girls settled back to watch the show going on outside. It was a good day.

MEW 14

Boo-Boo walked into the bedroom and seeing Gloria packing a suitcase asked, "What are you doing, Momma?"

"Kayla and I are going away for a few days. Remember, I told you the other day."

"Yes, I remember, but why?"

"Kayla got tickets to a show for her and I to see this Friday."

"What about Daddy?" and as soon as those words went out, Boo-Boo's mouth dropped, and her eyes got big. "Whoa, hold it, what about me and my sisters?"

"You have nothing to worry about. Daddy will be here to take care of all of you. It's only for a few days anyway. We leave this afternoon and we'll be back on Sunday."

"Does he know where our food is? Does he know when to feed us? What about our litter box? Who will clean that?"

"Yes. Yes. And for your litter box. Daddy. Daddy will take care of all of you while I am gone."

"We will need a phone to call you, Momma. Where can we get a phone?"

"Oh, now you're acting silly. You will be fine. Ted-D will be here to help Daddy take care of you, too."

"Oh good. I feel better now."

"I'm right here," a voice from behind Boo-Boo said.

Boo-Boo turned around to see Don in the bedroom doorway. "Well, you can't blame me for being fearful, can you, Daddy?"

"Well, no I can't. But that was a wee bit overdone now, wasn't it?"

"I was simply stressing the importance of the matter at hand," Boo-Boo replied with a grin.

"Understood," Daddy replied. "Now, let us leave your mother to her packing so as she doesn't forget anything." To Gloria, Don asked, "Can we take care of their nails before you leave, Love?"

"Yes, of course we can. I'm glad you said something about them. They are getting a bit sharp now, aren't they?"

Fifteen minutes later found Gloria and Don in the kitchen, Gloria with the nail trimmer and Don with the first one in his arms to have her nails clipped.

"I really can't believe how good you girls are when it comes to nail clipping time," Don said as he put Boo-Boo on the floor. "Who's next?"

Yogie ran over and Don picked her up; then Nellie and finally Marbles. Once all had their nails clipped, Gloria asked, "OK, who would like a treat?"

The four girls ran over to the counter where Gloria kept their treat jar and pranced around Gloria's feet.

"Well, it looks like everyone would like a treat. How about Daddy?"

The girls looked up at Don who promptly turned down the offer. "It's all theirs, Love. All theirs." With that, Don left the kitchen to the girls and Momma.

A few hours later, waving bye-bye to Momma and Kayla from the bay window, everyone watched Kayla drive away. With Momma.

Marbles turned around and asked, "So, when do we get fed Daddy?"

"Yes, Daddy," chimed in Boo-Boo, tongue hanging out and dragging it flat out on the floor, "I don't think I can make it much longer," she mumbled.

"Well, from what I'm seeing, I would say right about now," and off to the kitchen they went, Daddy and Ted-D in the lead, parade style.

Leaving the girls to eat, Ted-D went into the living room to spend some time with Little Kitty and Don went back into the office where, a short time later, he heard, "burp." Turning around he saw that Nellie had rambled on in and was sitting on Billie.

"What are you working on Daddy?"

"Music stuff. Trying to memorize something that is called two, five, one. It is used in a lot of music."

"Aren't you a wee bit too old to have to learn new stuff?"

"No one is ever too old to learn something new, Nellie. It's fun, well, for the most part, to learn new stuff."

"Well, I wish you lots of luck, Daddy. I mean, it can't be easy. You seem to be working on that an awful lot."

"Nothing worth learning is really easy, but it is usually worth the time and effort to learn. No matter what it is. Also, that is not the only thing I'm trying to learn in music. Doug has me learning a lot of stuff: scales, Blues, Jazz. Even though I've played saxophone for many years there is an awful lot I still don't know. I am so fortunate that Doug has the patience he does."

"I'm sure you'll learn everything he is teaching you. You're smart, Daddy."

"Well, thank you, Nellie. Now, I see you have noticed Billie is out again. So, what are you doing with Billie there?"

"Nothing, just tugging at her softness. And, well, getting my nails into her a bit."

"No. Don't do that, Nellie. What did we talk about last time, hmm? You'll hurt her and she won't be the same, having been all ripped apart."

"OK, Daddy. I'll stop."

But no matter how much Nellie tried to stop, she did not have the capability to do such and Don had to scold her.

"Now, now, I am going to have to put Billie away until you get a bit older. Then we will bring Billie back out and see how gentle you can be with her then."

"I'm sorry, Daddy. I tried."

"It's OK. Being a kitten is all about learning, too."

"Just like you learn music?"

"Yes, just like I learn music, too." Don smiled at Nellie as she got off Billie. Then Don rolled Billie up and put her in a safe spot.

A few days later, Ted-D sprang up from the couch and ran to the kitchen, jumped up on the counter and raced to the window in the kitchen.

"I thought so! I thought so! I heard Kayla stopping in front of the house. Momma and Kayla are home."

The four kittens ran to the window to check things out. Sure enough, there was Momma and Kayla getting out of the car, Momma with her suitcase in hand. Everyone ran to the door and opened it, waiting for Momma and Kayla to come in.

"We missed you," Ted-D screamed at the top of his lungs.

"Yes, we all missed you," the four kitties said in somewhat of a group near unison.

"Hi, Love, Kitten. Did you two have fun?"

"Yes, but lots of people. Still, it was a good time."

"What about you, Kitten? Did you have fun?"

"Sure. OK. Yea, I guess."

"Well, I'm glad to hear all positive things being said. How was traffic?"

"You know, busy," Kayla replied.

"I'm just glad to be back home. It's nice to go away, but I really do like being home."

"I completely understand, Love. At least you two had fun."

"That we did."

"Guess what, Momma?" Yogie quietly asked.

"What?"

"Daddy gave us extra food at mealtime." Yogie smiled. She may be a quiet one, in a sort of Janis Joplin looking way, but she could get in a word or two before her sisters said stuff at times.

"He did? Why?" Gloria looked at Don.

"Daddy got us the wrong food at night, so he decided to just give us each a can of food. Don't worry, we did not waste it. We ate it."

"Yes, we did," Nellie said in agreement. "Mmmmm."

"Just the first night, Love. I had opened all the little cans of food before realizing they were for the next two mornings, that the big cans were for at night. I told you I needed written directions."

"Oh, Honey, it's alright. I know you did the best you could."

"Oh, now you're just picking on me, aren't you?"

"Yes. Yes, I am." Gloria laughed.

"Doesn't matter. I still love you, Love."

"And I still love you, Honey."

"Uh-oh! Close your eyes, sisters. Momma and Daddy are going to get all kissy and huggy now."

"Get on my back, Ted-D. We'll head for the far end of the house, into our room to watch critters."

"Sounds like a plan, Marbles."

And off Ted-D rode, into the sunset on Marbles, with all his sisters in tow.

***

MEW 15

Walking past the girl's room, Don saw Nellie scratching on the tower-of-power's scratching post.

Nellie was so occupied that she was startled when Don spoke. "What's up, my Nellie buddy? You look like you're getting rid of a bit of tension there."

Nellie continued scratching as she replied to Don. "Daddy, I'm getting fat. Marbles is getting thinner and I'm getting fatter. I don't like it."

"Well, you are correct. You are getting bigger."

"Oh, no. You've noticed, too?" Nellie dug her nails deeper into the post.

"Yes, I have. There's nothing wrong with that. You must remember, it's our personalities that make us likeable; not how we look."

"You're just saying that because you've got a belly, too."

"Hey now. Let's not make this personal buddy. As for me, I don't mind at all. Sure, I'd like to be thinner and wear nicer clothes, but that's not going to happen. I like to eat. I don't like to exercise."

"Yea, me neither. I mean, I do like to chase my sisters and play with Ted-D, but that's all in fun."

"Exactly. So, you've got a choice to make but it seems you already have. So, be happy with who you are, my pudgy buddy." Daddy laughed out loud. "And I can be your pudgy Daddy. How about that?"

"I think we can do that."

At that, Nellie stopped scratching and raised her arms for Don to pick her up, which he did. He also topped it off with a hug.

"I love you, Daddy."

"And I love you, Nellie." Don gave Nellie a bear hug and then it seemed as if he stopped moving. He heard Nellie's heart beating. It was a bittersweet moment then as he realized he was standing in the last spot that he had heard

Alec's heart stop beating. The thump . . . thump . . .thump. . . and then quiet.

"Are you OK, Daddy? What's wrong?"

"I just recalled this is where Alec had passed, I had heard her last heart beats right here."

"I'm sorry to have brought that memory back, Daddy."

"Nothing for you to be sorry about, Nellie. That is life. If she had not been such a good girl, the pain would not be so hard to bear. But she was a good girl and that is why we have you and your sisters now. Had Alec been a not-so-good girl I don't think your mother and I would have given a thought to having kitties again."

Nellie gave Don a big hug.

"Just remember Daddy, I am not taking Alec's spot. I am only carrying on her love with my own."

"I know that, Nellie. I know that."

Nellie snuggled closer to Don's chest and, looking up, smiled. "The important thing is that we enjoy life as we do. With one another, with love."

***

MEW 16

"Good morning, ladies."

"Good morning, Daddy. Where's Momma? Is she up yet?"

"Yes, I am," Momma yelled into the living room, "I'll be right there."

"What's going on, Daddy? I feel like something is different today."

"You and your sisters will know as soon as your mother is here."

"Is it a surprise?" asked Yogie. "I like surprises." Yogie rolled onto her back, stretching her legs out and waited for someone to give her a belly rub.

While giving Yogie a belly rub, Momma answered Yogie's question, "I would think it may be a surprise today. We'll know soon enough. Now let us gather in the living room as we ask you a question."

Yogie jumped up to join her sisters on the couch. Momma sat in her chair as Daddy continued to stand by the hallway.

"OK, Momma, the suspense is just killing us. What is the surprise?"

"Oh my, it hasn't even been a minute, and the unknown is getting you all fidgety? How about if we talk a little bit first." Momma smiled as she slowly asked, "How was your sleep? Did you all have sweet dreams?"

Yogie, who rarely ever gets excited as such began jumping up and down, answering Momma's question with, "Yes, we all had sweet dreams. Best sweet dreams ever. They lasted all night, and no one wet their beds where ever they slept. Now what is the surprise?"

Daddy and Momma could not contain their laughter at Yogie's reply. Also, the way Yogie's sisters stared at her in amazement.

"Wow! Where did that come from, Yogie?" asked Marbles.

"I don't know. It scared me though."

"Nothing wrong with what you did, Yogie. Nothing at all. We know you're excited to learn what the surprise is, so, here it is. Are you ready?"

Nellie answered for her and her sisters, "Yes, we are Momma."

"OK, then. Does anyone know what today is?"

The room got very quiet as each looked at the other. Then they all shrugged their shoulders and quietly said, "No. No we don't Momma."

From behind Daddy Ted-D yelled, "I know what today is. I know. I know." And with that he jumped out from behind Daddy. "Can I tell them Momma, can I?"

"Yes, you may tell them, Ted-D."

"It's July 10th. Your first birthday!" Ted-D proudly exclaimed.

"Our birthday? Already? Oh wow! It's our birthday!" Yogie began to dance as Ted-D started to sing Happy Birthday to his sisters, Momma and Daddy joining in, too.

"Wow. We are officially one year old today. Oh my. I feel so old."

"Now, now Marbles. You are just beginning to age, just beginning. Enjoy it."

"I know, Daddy. I was just kidding." Marbles began to sing herself. "It's our birthday today, we are one year old. It's our birthday today, yay, yay, yay!"

"That was wonderful," Ted-D complimented Marbles. "I never knew you could sing so nice."

"I didn't either. Thank you big brother."

The rest of the day found the whole family enjoying the girl's birthday together. First, of course, there were the gifts. Of which the wrapping paper and boxes were more fun than the actual gifts. Yet, as time went on, those toys, the catnipped laced stuffed rat and such, well, they would be enjoyed for many months. At least until Christmas came around again.

As the day came to a close and the girls settled into nap time, because, as we all know, cats don't sleep through the whole night, well, as they settled into nap time, Yogie called out to Momma, Daddy, and Ted-D. "Thank you for everything today. That was a nice surprise."

"You're welcome. You girls mean the world to your Daddy, Ted-D and I. You and your sisters are gifts each day to us. Thank you."

"Oh Momma. You spoil us so much."

"Now, now, time for naps, OK? We love you all. Sweet dreams."

"Sweet dreams, Momma."

MEW 17

"What's that thing?" Boo-Boo asked from her place on Don's lap.

"This here is what I had bought when Alec would sit on my lap whilst I typed away on old QWERTY. It is to be used to clear the boogers out of children's noses but I use it to blow kitty hair off my monitors so I can see clearly now."

"I like the color," Boo said. "It's pretty."

"I didn't know you could see colors. I guess I never thought of it."

"Yes, some colors. Blue is my favorite." Boo-Boo smiled. "If you say blue two times it's like my name." Boo-Boo laughed.

Don joined in with a laugh, too. How could he not?

At that moment, a raucous began in the girl's room, continuing into the hallway and into the office by Boo-Boo and Don. It was Nellie.

"What's wrong, buddy?" Don asked.

"Come. Come quick, Daddy. You must stop them. You must stop them!!!"

"Who? Stop who?"

"Hurry, Daddy. Come quick. Hurry." And with that Nellie raced back to her room.

Don looked down at Boo-Boo who was as wide-eyed as Don, and with an "OK, Boo-Boo, here we go" they both got up and walked briskly to the girl's room.

Upon entering they found Nellie on the desk peering out the window along with Marbles and Yogie. Dust was coming into the open window and they all had tears in their eyes.

"What is going on out there, girls?"

"The trees, Daddy. The trees." Nellie whimpered.

"They are cutting the trees down, Daddy. Never more shall we enjoy their beauty," Marbles said.

"The trees never did anything bad, Daddy. Never," Yogie softly stated. "They were trees. Giving homes to the chipmunks, the squirrels. . ." Yogie's words trailed off in sadness.

"Shade to the bunnies," Nellie interjected.

"And privacy between us and the neighbors across the lot," Daddy said, hanging his head low.

"Make them stop, Daddy. Make them stop."

"I wish I could, Nellie, girls. I wish I could." Don's words came out slow and sorrowful. "But it is the neighbor's yard to do as the neighbor sees fit, not as you or I see."

"Or anyone else." It was Marbles who said that. "You see, if it does not hurt the city, or make things look bad, no one cares what one does to their own property. It is theirs to do as they wish."

Daddy agreed, "Marbles is correct. I wish she wasn't, but she is. It is no different than when we cut down the trees in the backyard."

"Yes, it is different," Nellie was defiant, getting up on her paws, wiping the tears from her eyes. "Those trees were unsafe. They were past their life expectancy and were ready to fall. These trees out our window were not going to fall! And in a few months they were going to show their beautiful colors."

"I understand what you are saying, Nellie. Still, there is nothing we can do."

"I wish we could buy that lot from him. Then we could plant new trees."

Yogie sat up straighter, hope in her eyes. "Yes, Daddy, let's buy that from our neighbor and plant trees. Give the critters their homes again; their shade."

"I wish we could, Yogie. But unless our next book sells millions of copies, I don't see that happening."

"It will happen, Daddy. It will happen."

Daddy turned to face Marbles. "Do you know something that we don't, Marbles?"

"One must have positive thoughts, beliefs. And if it does not happen, we are still doing better than had we not tried."

"You are so deep in your words at times. I appreciate it, Marbles."

"You are quite welcome, Daddy. I only say what comes to my mind."

"Now what do we do, Daddy?" asked Yogie.

"I hate to say it, but not much we can do. We can only hold onto the memories," replied Daddy.

"Isn't there anything we can do for the critters? I mean, we can't just leave them without a home, can we?" asked Nellie.

Again, Marbles being the wise one answered, "We are in no position to get them new homes, but we can at least make sure they have the strength to obtain their new homes."

"What do you mean?" Daddy asked.

"Let us put extra food out for them so they may have full strength to make new homes."

"And fresh clean water?" Yogie piped in.

"Yes, that is a grand idea," Daddy smiled.

"This way they will also know that we have not left them to fend for themselves. That we love them," Nellie proclaimed.

"Oh, that is so wrong," Momma said as she walked into the room and spied what was taking place out the window. "Why would he do that to those critters?"

"Only one answer, Love. Money. I really did not think he would have the trees cut down. I mean he did not like it when the city cut down trees by his house. He was irate. And now..."

"This." Marbles finished Daddy's sentence.

"Yes. Now this." Daddy emphasized.

"Nothing we can do about it either. It's his land. He can do whatever he wants with it and there's nothing we can say or do about it either," Momma said as she wiped a tear from her cheek. "I'm just afraid that we will lose the nature that we had living around us. That and our privacy. Oh my, just look how we can see the neighbors."

"And, the neighbors can see us," Daddy said. "Well, you know we always find a work around. We will just have to figure this one out, too."

"Can we plant some trees in the backyard for the birdies, Daddy?" asked Marbles.

"That is a grand idea, Marbles. Yes, we can find something that will work. We don't have a lot of room anymore, but we will find something that will work."

"And the bunnies and chipmunks? The squirrels, too?" asked Boo-Boo.

"We will figure out something for all involved," Momma stated. "Not all is lost. Well, except our privacy by the windows."

"Love, I can find some tint and tint the east windows. That is, if you don't mind."

"Can you do that? Could we still see out?"

"Yes. There is tint that I can put on the windows where we can see out, but no one can see in. Except for at night, but then we will have the curtains closed."

"That would be wonderful, Honey. Thank you."

"You're welcome, Love. It won't be what we were used to, nor the critters, but it is better than what this situation is giving us as is."

"True that," Nellie said. "True that."

Before any of them had a chance to blush, Boo-Boo shouted, "Hey, Yogie kicked poo out of the litter box."

The three sisters and Daddy turned to look at Yogie.

"Are you thinking about our neighbor?" Boo-Boo jokingly asked.

"All I can say is sh-."

Daddy interrupted. "No, you can't say it." And with that, their laughter broke some tension in the room.

"You girls amaze me."

"Why is that, Momma?" they asked in unison.

"How you all came together to help others in need. I am so proud of you."

Ted-D came in at that moment to see what was going on, having been woken from his nap. As Daddy went back to his office to continue writing the new book and Momma to her tasks in the living room, Ted-D's sisters began to tell their brother about what had taken place and how they were going to help the critters, their friends, by making sure they were well fed and watered. Love abounded.

***

MEW 18

The calendar pages flipped, and the day came along that all feared, but had to get past. The one-year anniversary of Alec-the-Cat's passing.

Not much was said. Enough, but not too much to where one would dwell upon it. Alec was a great companion; a great friend and she would never be forgotten. And with that . . .

"Nellie. Hey, Nellie buddy. You want to come into the office for a bit?"

Nellie rolled over, facing away from the sun that she was basking in, and yelled back to Daddy, "Right after I stretch," and a short time later walked into the office.

"What's up, Daddy?"

"I thought we'd give it another try," Daddy said with a smile.

"Give what another try?" As she spoke the words, she followed Don's gaze to where he was looking. There, in front of the fireplace, lies Billie. "Billie," Nellie shouted in excitement. "How are you doing?" Nellie went to lie upon Billie's softness.

"Yes. Billie. I thought you might be to the point of being responsible for her now. Now that you're a bit older and wiser."

"Aww, Daddy. Thank you." Nellie rolled around on Billie. "I will make sure to take good care of her. Just like Alec did."

"I know you will. Alec would like that. Keep in mind that you will need to share Billie with your sisters, too."

"I will, Daddy. And Ted-D, too." Nellie snuggled in the softness of Billie, giving her a hug in the process. "Oh, Billie. I missed you."

**

MEW 19

Closing the door behind him, Don yelled into the house, "Well, here we go again."

Gloria yelled back in reply, "I can't hear you, I'm in the girls' room." A minute later, she appeared in the kitchen. "What did you say, Honey?"

"Here we go again."

"Here we go again, what?"

"They've decided to change my hours at work. Again."

"Again? What are they trying to do, get rid of you? They've already pushed out so many. No one with any knowledge will be left."

"I believe that is what they are trying to do. My so-called supervisor, Simpleton, even told me himself he'd like to get rid of me."

"You mean, Mr. Simpleton. Now, now, Honey, show some respect."

"You are correct, Love. He has earned Mr. in front of that name."

Gloria hid a smile and continued, "Well, that doesn't surprise me at all. Then he would have a chance to look like he might know something."

"Highly doubtful. He reminds me of Michael Scott on that show, *The Office*. As you know, they only put him in that position because his supervisor needed a whipping boy. He himself has no clue what to do."

"I can't wait until you put your papers in to retire, Honey. I really don't know why you have stayed this long. Except for the insurance. At least your sixty-two now."

"Exactly. I keep hoping it will change for the better, but it's lost. I only hope to get out before they close the place down. And at this rate, it won't be long. There's almost 150 of us that can retire before the next contract. And that's less than two years away."

"I believe you better get to calling your retirement in, Honey. It's time."

"Yes. You are correct. It is time. And, according to my spreadsheets, if I'm only losing forty dollars a month in retirement, heck, I'll make up for that in the fact I won't be needing gas, nor the wear and tear on the truck, for going back and forth to work."

"Then do it. Today."

"Yes. You are probably correct. I best do it before the influx of others trying to retire. I'll be in the office getting things together. Thanks, Love. Oh, what about supper? What should I make?"

"Don't worry about that. I'll go get us something to eat. Would you like Culver's or something else?"

"Culver's is good. Thanks, Love."

Once in the office, Don opened his briefcase to get his computer up and running. The first thing he noticed was the packet of info about the weld department that he was put in charge of taking care of, unbeknownst to others.

"Guess all this does not matter anymore. They can keep that problem child in charge at night and deal with it themselves. Gloria's right. It's time."

"It's time for what, Daddy?"

Don turned around to see Nellie walking up into the office.

"Oh, was I talking out loud?"

"It's OK, Daddy. We're used to it." Nellie came closer, rubbing against Don's leg and asked again, "Time for what?"

"Time to retire."

"Retire? From what? You're away from home job?" Nellie sounded excited.

"That's correct, my buddy. Momma's rarely wrong, so I must listen to her on this matter, too. It's time."

"I agree," Nellie purred.

"You agree, too?"

"Yes. I miss seeing you. I mean it's one thing when you are working from home, at least I see you once in a while throughout the day, but when you are working all those hours at that other place, well, I don't like it. I miss you, Daddy."

"Awww, come here, my pudgy, little, Nellie buddy." Picking Nellie up Don cuddled her in his arms. At that moment, coming from the kitchen stereo, a song played. A slow song. Don began to rock back and forth, slow dancing with Nellie, who seemed to be enjoying the moment.

The song got done, the DJ spun another, and Don put Nellie back down on the floor.

"That was nice, Daddy."

"I thought so, too. If only Seth MacFarlane knew he got some cool cats to dance to his music, I bet he'd be proud."

"Really, Daddy?

"Why not?"

"Yes, why not?" Nellie laughed. "I better let you get to filling out those retirement papers now. But, one question, Daddy?

"Yes. What's that?"

"Aren't you going to miss the people in your office? I mean, you saw them like forever."

"Yes, I will miss them. They were like family at times."

"Even Jeremy?" Nellie asked, puzzled.

"Yes, even Jeremy. Just because we didn't see eye-to-eye on work issues most of the time, didn't make him a bad person."

"So, one should take into consideration all parts of the equation before coming to a conclusion?"

"Very well put, Nellie. Very well put."

"I love you, Daddy."

"I love you too, Nellie."

At that moment of warmed hearts Yogie came barreling into the room. Putting on the breaks, she slid into Don's ankles whilst at the same time asking, "What about Debbie?"

"Debbie?" asked Don.

"Yes," Yogie said gleefully. "You know, Little Debbie. She has a cat named Milo and is cute like me."

"Yes, of course I'll miss Little Debbie. How could I not?"

"I don't know, Daddy. It would be terrible if you forgot about her."

"I will remember each one of them. No doubt."

"Even Christa?" Asked Boo-Boo roughly as she came around the corner. "I mean, she does have Baily."

"And your point is?" asked Don.

Boo-Boo put a paw near her mouth and whispered, "Baily is a D-O-G."

Don couldn't help but laugh a bit. "You are correct in that Baily is a D-O-G, but that does not mean I would want to forget about Christa. Dogs are beautiful animals, too.

Just like people, animals come in all shapes, colors, sizes, ---."

"Yes, we know, Daddy. We should love all mankind and all creatures unless of course, they have done something terribly wrong," Marbles replied as if her voice was on a trampoline bouncing up and down.

"That is correct, Marbles."

"So, if that means we should like dogs, then I am under the impression you are not going to forget Thom?"

"Simpleton?" Don cleared his throat. "I mean, Thom is no different than a dog, Marbles."

"How so, Daddy?"

"Some dogs you can get close and pet, others you cannot. Those are the ones that you don't want to forget either, because they will lash out. Many don't even know why they do it, but we remember those times and learn from them. That is why I won't forget Thom. Instead, I pity him."

"Thom's a dog. Thom's a dog." The girls all chanted, laughing so hard they sounded like they were hacking up a hairball, which, well, Marbles did.

***

MEW 20

It was early morning when Don awoke to the sound of someone getting sick. It was one of the girls, and it sounded like it was coming from the hall. He thought about waking Gloria up, but he then remembered she had already gotten up to go to work. Maybe she was in the bathroom yet?

Getting up to check, he was disappointed that she had already left for work. Oh well, he could take care of this himself. Man up, man!

Getting his phone to use the flashlight on there, he headed for where the sound of hacking had come. Finding Nellie standing guard over the wet spot, not knowing if it was her or one of her sisters, Don was relieved to find out there wasn't much to clean up.

"That I'll leave up to you two. Just keep in mind, no eating when you go up to the bowls, just point. This way we won't take any chances of something being in the food and with you only pointing, no one else will hear which bowl it is that you ate from."

"Or bowls," Nellie said.

"That is correct."

"Now, what about Marbles and Yogie? Don't we need them to tell us which bowls they ate from?"

"Good question, Boo-Boo. I was thinking that since they aren't getting sick that we did not need to know that, but that is a good point. Yes, we will have each of them then go into the room and show me which bowls they have eaten out of, just to make sure it is not the same ones you two have eaten from."

"What if they are the same ones, Daddy?" asked Nellie.

"Well, if they are the same bowls then we know that it isn't the food. There must be another root cause to this sickness."

"Root cause?" asked Marbles.

"Yes, root cause. The very basis of any cause-and-effect issue. What is the main thing that has triggered this event? In this case, your sisters getting sick."

"Interesting. I have learned something new."

"Nothing wrong with learning something new, is there?"

"Oh no," Marbles replied. "I'm all for learning as much as I can." She smiled.

"Me, too," Don said.

After Marbles went to get Yogie, who was already looking out their window and enjoying the day, Daddy spoke, "OK, girls, let us begin. Everybody except the one going into the room to pick out their food eaten today and myself will be in that room. When your sister is done showing me what she has eaten, then she will leave and tell the next one to go on in. The staging area will be the living room, and I will be in the hallway watching into your room, so as to give you space and no pressure to recall your routine of today. Sound good?"

All four looked up at Daddy and gave their high paws in agreement. Nellie went first, leaving the others to wait. When each had their turn, they all gathered in the living room, Ted-D too, for the results of their experiment.

"Ok, Daddy, did they eat the same food?" asked Ted-D.

Don looked up from his clipboard, looking all official, and stated that four out of four of them had indeed eaten out of the same bowls.

"So, why are not all of my sisters getting sick?" Ted-D asked puzzled.

"Well, Ted-D, two of your sisters ate out of the same bowls while two of your other sisters ate out of two different bowls. Marble and Yogie ate out of bowls one and three while Boo-Boo and Nellie ate out of bowls two and four."

"So, that means it could be the food?"

"Yes, that is what it is looking like. So now I will take bowls two and four and put them in the sink for Momma to look at. Maybe she can see something we don't."

"Great idea, Daddy. Now, sisters, do not eat out of the bowls that Daddy puts in the sink, OK?"

After Daddy put the bowls in the sink, he sat down in the living room and huddled with the girls and Ted-D.

"I sure don't get in this room a lot. It's kind of a new room to me." Daddy smiled.

"We like it when you spend time like this with us. It's rare, usually it is only one or two of us at a time, not all four of us and Ted-D. This is nice."

"Yes, it is nice Marbles. I sure can't wait until the projects are done. Or at least at a good place on the list, no pressures or must do's."

"Now that your retired Daddy, you'll have more time to get things done."

"That's true, Ted-D. But I sure don't move like I used to."

"You do good, Daddy. You do good."

"I remember when you weren't sure about being retired," Nellie said. "You were kind of lost."

"I know. It was a whole different routine. Not having to go to work and yet, still worried about if things were getting done as they should there."

"But Daddy, there are other people in your office to take care of those things."

"Well, most of those things, but I was also over-seeing a few special projects that no one else in my office was aware of, much less the front office."

"You were?"

"Yes, Ted-D. I had been asked many years ago to take on a project because of my background. And with the extra perks that were offered, I could not see saying no. Now they have someone at another company taking over what I had done."

"But you are happy that you are retired, aren't you, Daddy?

"For sure, Ted-D. For sure. My blood pressure has been getting better, as are my headaches."

"But you still think about work?"

"Basically, it is the people whom I had worked with that I miss the most. I mean I have jokes to tell and no one to tell them to."

"Don't you talk with them anymore, Daddy?"

"Well, I had for a while, but as time moved on, so did we all. They have their world; I now have mine."

"That's too bad." Ted-D crawled over to Don and put his arms around Don's neck, giving him a big old teddy bear hug and into Don's ear whispered, "You can always tell me your jokes, Daddy."

With a tear peeking out, Don hugged Ted-D a bit tighter. "That means a lot, Ted-D. Thank you."

"You're welcome, Daddy. We are all here for you."

"Life. Sometimes it gets in the way of living."

Don looked down to see that Marbles had entered the room. "That is true, Marbles. Very true. But I believe we are all very lucky to be together. And I love that."

"I must confess something," Marbles said.

"What's that?" Daddy asked as he petted her head, she having now laid on Don's leg, the others each taking a spot where they could in the recliner where they all sat.

"For quite some time, I was worried."

"About what?"

"Well, Daddy, I was thrilled that you and Momma had adopted me and my sisters, but I was worried it would not last. That we would eventually branch off to different homes."

"Why would you think that?"

"Well, with the cost of food and litter. I mean, we are a handful."

"Now, now Marbles. I too must also confess something. And that is I never gave a thought to the cost of those items, and as time went on, I saw how much they did cost. Still, if needed, I would have stayed up around the clock writing books if that is what it would had taken to keep you and your sisters safe and taken care of, from food to litter. Momma would have done something similar, too. We love you all. You are family."

"Thank you, Daddy. That makes me feel secure."

"You're welcome, Marbles. I hope that makes everybody feel secure." At that there were smiles and actual meows and purrs. Ted-D jumped off the top of the recliner, springing over Don's shoulders and onto an arm of the recliner.

"You're my sisters," Ted-D exclaimed. "And if need be, I would have taken every last bit of food out of your food cans, so we did not throw any of it away."

"Really?" asked Boo-Boo. "Wouldn't that have gotten all over your paws?"

"Yes, but that is how much I love all of you. And anyway, I'm sure none of you would have minded helping me clean up." Ted-D laughed at his little joke as the others nodded in agreement and laughed at themselves.

"Now," Ted-D continued, "each of you seem to have a special spot that you claim as your own."

"We do?" asked Boo-Boo.

"Yes," Ted-D replied. "You, my sister Boo-Boo, likes to be at the top of the tower-of-power scratching post, Yogie loves to sleep on the kitchen counter, Nellie waits for Daddy on his briefcase in his office, and Marbles likes to sit on guard near the treat cabinet."

"I do like my treats," agreed Marbles with a smile.

"I remember how sad we were to leave our first home," Yogie shared. "But we are very happy to be with you and Momma. And as a bonus, we have a big brother in Ted-D and a big sister in Kayla Kitten. Yay!"

Ted-D yelled out, "Group hug" and they all came together for the house's biggest teddy bear hug yet. And then, from amongst the hug-a-thon, Boo-Boo said. . .

"I don't feel too well." And just like that, they all scattered like the break of pool balls done by Minnesota Fats.

***

MEW 21

Saturday morning found Don in his office, writing this book. It was early. Very early. 11:00 A.M. early!

With a pot of coffee perked, two cups removed and processed with a third serving sitting within reach, Don attempted to put words into the shape of a story. Instead, he yawned. And yawned again.

Don heard something behind him, coming from near the door. He noticed Nellie attempting to squeeze through the cat door, effort paying off slowly.

"I knew you could do it, buddy."

Nellie looked up at Don in his chair and hissed, "You could maybe, somehow, anytime you have time on your hands, maybe, possibly, could you make that door bigger?" Nellie pleaded.

"I could but then it would look like a train tunnel for your sisters and I'm afraid they would get lost."

"Funny. Very not funny."

Don laughed despite being himself. "Sorry, buddy. I couldn't resist."

"I only consider the source, Daddy. I learned that from you." Nellie laughed. "What are you doing up so early?"

"I need to finish this book. Soon. With everything going on all at once, I just don't seem to have the normal time to write anymore."

"You mean, later in the day?"

"That is correct. It seems that as soon as I get one issue taken care of, another comes in to fill the void. Then, of course, I've got new music to constantly learn for upcoming concerts."

"You do like that, though, don't you, Daddy?"

"You mean all the things I need to take care of?"

"No, I mean the new music."

"Yes, of course I do. It gives me an escape from the daily responsibilities. Still, it does take time away from writing."

"I believe what is taking time away from your writing is all the other things you do."

"Yes, but the things that I'm doing like planting of the trees, putting a new roof on the shop, etc. etc. all need to be done."

"I do understand that, Daddy. But once those are done, I have heard you say that your list of "things to do" is getting smaller and smaller. That should mean you will have more time to write and to enjoy playing new music."

"Yes, you are correct. And I am so much looking forward to being able to do that. But as of this moment, I do need to get this book finished. I have readers contacting me from all over the world asking when this book is going to be on sale. Yet, I can't seem to find the words to put in this book now."

"I am sure some of the reason for that is the stress that you and Momma are going through with Uncle Wayne's passing. I know you two are burning the candle trying to empty his house sooner than later, trying to get it done before the snow falls."

"Yes, that is taking a toll upon us. First, Wayne was my buddy who I had thought I would be spending more time with now that I retired. So, yes, that breaks my heart. Those tears you see being shed every now and then from myself and Momma are for the unmade memories of tomorrow that we will never have together with Wayne.

Second, it is very hard on your momma. Wayne's home was a second home for when your momma was growing up and, well, all the way until Wayne passed. He and Aunt Bev were like second parents to your mother. And now to watch her decide what to keep and what to donate, and worse, what to put in the dumpster because of all the smoke damage caused by Bev and Wayne's smoking? It does stress her out as well as me. It is not easy, but we all go through it and must continue living." Don sat back in his chair and looked out the window, the grey skies of winter teasing him from afar.

"Daddy, why don't you sit back and listen to me? I will tell you a story and you do the typing. Together we will get this book written and the readers will love it."

"Seriously? How can you just tell me a story?"

"The same way I've seen you write a story. I have experience, too."

"Well, OK. I guess, I suppose."

"No guessing, no supposing, Daddy. Now, oil up those QWERTY hammers and let's get this book finished."

With that, Don turned from the window, faced the computer, and poised his fingers at the keyboard. Nellie jumped up on the desk and brushed her tail against a few items, making way for her to get comfortable.

Looking up at Don, Nellie cleared her throat, "Let us begin my chapter."

Don nodded. Nellie began to speak; Don began to type.

***

MEW 22

"Servant. Servant. I'm done." It was Nellie doing the beckoning.

Arriving at the door to Nellie's room, Don leaned in and out of breath said, "Yes, Princess Nellie. You are done. But you did not say done with what."

"Take a sniff and you shall know what I am done with. I am not about to broadcast it to thy neighbors."

Without thinking, Don took in a whiff of air into his nostrils. Wrong thing to do. Nellie laughed as Don's eyes watered.

"You may attend to the cleaning of, ahem, my "debris". I shall go into your bedroom and take a nap. The actions of the past few minutes have made me quite tired. I gather you have left the bed unmade since you arose this morning?"

"Yes, Princess Nellie. Just as you like it, unmade and with the softest of the blankets heaved up for you to noodle with when you wish. I have also made sure to leave the blue mouse within the second softest blanket in which you enjoy napping."

"Thank you, Servant. Now, if you do not mind," Nellie laughed. "Even if you do mind, no matter, I shall be taking my nap."

"Good night, Princess Nellie."

"Good night, Servant. Now, please make sure that you have cleaned the royal litter box and smoothed out the top that I may walk in next time as if I'm on a beautiful beach."

"I shall do as you request, Princess Nellie." Under his breath he continued, "So you can crap on the beautiful beach."

"Did you have a thought?"

"No. No thoughts. Well, there is one."

"What would that be, Servant?"

"I was wondering which can of food my Princess would like to be waiting for her when she awakes?"

"Tuna. Tuna Supreme would be lovely."

With that, Nellie, . . . Princess Nellie, went off to nap while Don retrieved the royal scooper.

Hours later, Don heard Nellie get up from her nap.

"You may retrieve my treats, Servant." Nellie put her front legs out and stretched.

Don knelt in front of Princess Nellie, took her paw in his hand and licked it. "It shall be with great delight that I am allowed to do so." He then rose to his feet and skipped off to the royal kitchen to get Princess Nellie her treats.

When he returned, he knelt near the bed, and, one by one, fed Nellie her treats. As she finished her last morsal she proceeded to hack it all back up.

"Oh my," she quipped. "Apparently, I have eaten too fast."

"So, I see, Princess," agreed Don. "Allow me to clean that misfortune up."

"Allow, I shall," Nellie said, backing away from her treat-catastrophe. "When you have finished, you may return with a bowl of water for me. My mouth is quite yucky from this event."

"I shall do as you request your Highness." And once again, Don skipped off, a forced smile barely seen.

Finishing a few laps from the water bowl Don had brought back to Princess Nellie, she then decided it was time to do her yoga.

"Servant, you may open thy curtains and allow the afternoon sun to caress my being. It is time for my yoga session."

"At once, your Highness."

"There, that is much better," stated Nellie, now lying on the floor entrenched within old Sol's rays of warmth.

Don watched from a distance as Nellie performed *her* half-moon, stretching to the stars while on her right side.

"Am I not something else?" she looked up at Don and asked.

"Yes, you are quite something else," Don agreed.

"I do like when you state true facts, it makes me happy."

"I am glad to hear that your Princess."

"I figured you would be. Now, I will need my belly rubbed. I am tired."

Don went to Nellie's side, sat down on the floor and rubbed her belly. Nellie purred. Don was the luckiest servant in the world.

All got quiet for a while then Nellie emphatically stated, "The end." Nellie smiled. "How's that for a story, Daddy?"

Don looked up from the keyboard in bewilderment.

"I cannot believe that you want this put into the new book. Any book for that matter!"

"Hey, you typed it," replied Nellie. "Use some imagination, Daddy. Haven't you ever used imagination, making believe something could really be when it simply could not be true?"

"Yes, I've tried it once or twice but people thought I was crazy, that I had gone mad."

"Well, you should use some imagination now. I mean, that was a very good story I just told you. Personally, I really liked it. Actually, I thought it was some of my best stuff."

"I thought it was going to get better, or have a twist, or, or something."

Nellie laughed. "Well, I spoke it so it must be true."

"True? How can that be true?" Don asked bewildered.

"Because I'm a cat and I spoke it. You do not know if there is another parallel universe that us cats may know about, do you, Daddy-O? Hmm?"

Don turned his head with a jerk and looked at Nellie. "Daddy-O?"

"That's what I said, Daddy." Nellie smiled and again asked Don, "Do you know if us cats have a parallel universe?"

"Five minutes ago, I would have said I don't believe that. Now?" Don took a deep breath and exhaled. "Now, I would believe it."

"So, my story stays in your book?"

"Yes, your story stays in the book. Thank you, Nellie."

Nellie purred as she got up. Walking towards Don, she put out a paw which Don took in his hand and rubbed.

"I love you, Nellie buddy." Don cleared his throat. "I mean, Princess Nellie."

Nellie smiled, and softly said, "I love you, too, Daddy." And with that, Nellie licked Don's hand, jumped off the desk and walked toward the cat door, leaving Don to re-read what he had just typed.

Before going out into the hallway though, Nellie looked back and said, "I can't wait until the book comes out. Hurry up, we have readers waiting."

Don rotated in his chair to face the monitor once again. In the background he heard, "Momma, I need a treat. I've been over-worked."

"That darn girl," Don said to himself, but inside he was laughing and warm with love for Nellie. "She's a good girl."

***

MEW 23

"What are you doing there, Ted-D?" Boo-Boo asked.

Ted-D was crawling around in the closet, moving this piece of clothing, then pushing that piece of clothing, all while looking like a miner in search of gold.

"I'm trying to decide what bow tie I should wear tonight."

"Wear? Why would you want to wear anything? Don't you like your body just the way it is?" Boo-Boo asked.

"Well, of course I like how I look." Then Ted-D thought it over for a second following up his answer with, "And even if I didn't, I couldn't do much about it, could I? After all I am whose I am." Ted-D laughed in spite of himself.

"Well, I suppose that is true. Yet, again I ask, why are you looking to dress up?"

Proudly, Ted-D replied, "Momma and Daddy are taking me to see a show tonight at the P.A.C. in Appleton. So, I get dressed up so as not to be the only one au naturel."

"The P.A.C. in Appleton. T==hat sounds like a mouth full." Boo-Boo rolled over and watched Ted-D scavenge around some more. "What is this P.A.C. in Appletown?"

Ted-D laughed and politely corrected his sister, "Appleton, not Appletown."

Boo-Boo laughed. "Oops. Appleton."

"Well, first Appleton is a place about an hour away from here. Once we arrive in Appleton, then we drive for a while into town and there is this big, beautiful building that is called the Performing Arts Center; P.A.C. for short. You know, abbreviated."

"Abbreviated?"

"That means to shorten up a lot of words instead of saying them and filling our mouths with all those letters."

"Oh, I think I know what you mean. So, Marbles could save a lot of time just by going by Momma and saying "MILIFITFMT?""

Ted-D looked at his sister like she was a bit crazy and asked, "MILIFITFMT?"

"Yes, MILIFITFMT. Momma, it's late. I'm famished. It's time for my treats."

"Well," Ted-D laughed, "Marbles could try it, but I'm not too sure if Momma would know what that meant."

"Yes, I suppose you are correct, Ted-D," Boo-Boo agreed. "I mean, that is an awful lot of letters filling up her mouth while it would be so much easier just to say the words. So, tell me about this P.A.C."

"It's a place for the performing arts. Musicals, stage plays, bands, singers, anything performing I suppose. Momma and Daddy took me to a lot of events there. Then we go to Five Guy's Burgers where they each get a burger, and I get to smell all the burgers. MMMMM." Ted-D drifted off into la-la-land with his thoughts.

"Ted-D, Ted-D!" Boo-Boo shook Ted-D back to reality. "So, what do you do at the P.A.C.?"

"Well, Momma and Daddy have season tickets, so we go to the same seats for all the shows during the year. But before the show starts, we sit outside, and people watch. That is always fun. Once in a while someone might even wave to me. Then Momma and Daddy will have a nice conversation with them telling them who I am, and that Daddy writes books and Momma edits them to make Daddy's words sound good."

Boo-Boo's eyes got big as a can of kitty food. "You mean complete strangers? Isn't that dangerous?"

"It could be if I was alone, but the people approach Momma and Daddy and talk with them first. You know, to make sure it is alright for them to wave to me. I mean, they don't hear me talk, they just think I'm cute and are wondering why they have me there with them at the shows. It's quite fun."

"Ah, yes. Not many people really open their hearts and their ears to hear any of us speak, do they? I have noticed many people really don't even listen to one another, always in a rush to say what is on their minds but really prefer not to listen to others. Quite sad it is."

"Yes, it is sad." Ted-D looked down.

"I'm so sorry. Please. Tell me what you do when Momma and Daddy get done visiting with these people."

Ted-D looked up and said, laughing as he did so, "Not much really. We go to our seats, watch the show, clap our hands and then go for burgers. Yet, it is still fun. The lights, music, costumes. It is so neat to see the talent they bring to the stage."

"That does sound really interesting and fun. And costumes? So that is why you dress up, too?"

"I suppose it is. I mean, I do like to look dapper every now and then myself." Ted-D giggled. "Hey, Boo-Boo, how about this one?" Ted-D held up a red polka dotted bow tie for Boo-Boo to see. "Do you think that will be good to wear tonight?"

Boo-Boo looked the bow tie over as Ted-D held it up. Then, having Ted-D put it down, Boo-Boo took her paw and spun it around and then she asked Ted-D to put it on.

"I'll need some help with that, if you don't mind."

"Oh, no problem." Boo-Boo took the bow tie into her mouth, walked behind Ted-D and, with a tug here and a tug there, wrestled it onto her brother. "There you go, Big Brother." Boo-Boo walked in front of Ted-D to see how the bow tie looked on him.

"Yes, yes, that does bring out the color of your being. Very nice, I mean, very dapper my big brother. Very dapper."

Ted-D blushed. "Thank you for helping me, Boo-Boo."

"No problem, Ted-D. We are here for each other."

***

MEW 24

Sitting at the desk, looking at his to-do list, Don heard a noise near him. It was Nellie, gently putting her nails into the leather chair, attempting to get his attention.

"What's up, buddy?"

"Sisters," she said with disgust.

Picking Nellie up, Don asked, "Sisters? What about your sisters?"

Nellie turned around in Don's lap and looked him straight in the eyes. "Why do I have them?"

"Well, I suppose it was either sisters or it was going to be brothers. It sounds like there's an issue going on here."

Stroking Nellie's back, Don asked, "Would you like to explain it to me, Nellie buddy?"

"One of my sisters puked all over Billie. Then they walked away."

"Well, I'll clean it up. I know how attached you have got with Billie. I think that is really neat since Alec also liked Billie quite a bit."

"Thanks, Daddy. I appreciate it. Still, why didn't they tell you they got sick on Billie? Instead, they just walked away, leaving their nasty puke in Billie's hair. It's just not right, Daddy."

"No, it's not, Nellie. Don't worry, I'll have a talk with them. They shouldn't be afraid of telling anyone if something happens. Good or bad."

"That's right. Instead, Billie laid there for who knows how long, looking all yucky. How could they do that?"

"Now, now, Nellie. We all get afraid at times."

"Even you, Daddy." Nellie cradled into Don's arms like a wee baby in a bassinette.

"Yes, even I get afraid at times. No one likes to look bad. Yet, it is part of life. None of us are perfect."

"Not even Momma?"

"Don't tell her I said this, but no, not even Momma."

Nellie's eyes got big as a pie tin. "Are you afraid of Momma, Daddy?"

"Let me say I have respect for your momma. Yet, she is a living creature, a human being, not a cat, even though she may think she is at times."

"She sure does like her paw socks, doesn't she, Daddy?" Nellie seemed to be relaxing a bit now.

"Yes, she does. But I have yet to see her run up to the top of your tower-of-power like you and your sisters do."

"Oh, Daddy, I don't think she would do that."

Daddy chuckled. "No, I suppose you are correct. Well, as I was saying, we all make bad calls at times. Do the wrong thing or say the wrong thing. We simply must get ourselves together and take responsibility for our actions or our words."

"Exactly! That's what I always do."

Don looked at Nellie in his lap and smiled. "It is, is it?"

"Yes, it is."

"I think you are forgetting something that just took place recently."

"What's that?" Nellie asked, licking her paw and rubbing it behind an ear.

Don reached for his coffee and took a sip of the go-go juice. Looking over the rim of the coffee cup, he asked, "You don't remember?"

Nellie stopped rubbing her ear and paused for a minute before answering, "Oh, yea. The soda on your desk." She did not look Don in the eyes as she said these words.

"That's correct. I came into the office last week only to find you and Boo-Boo on my desk, licking up soda that spilled out of the can I left sitting."

"We didn't mean to knock it over, Daddy. We tried to clean it up before you got back to the office."

"I know you girls tried your best. But again, hiding bad things is not going to make them disappear. I mean, how did you think you and your sister were to get the can to stand back up?"

"Magic?" Nellie joked.

Don laughed. "Yes, magic." He petted Nellie again. She and Don were the closest of all the kitties, but he loved each one of them in special ways. They all had their gifts, but Nellie and he just seemed to bond.

"Do you remember what else I said that day?"

"Yes, it surprised me and Boo-Boo when you stated that it was also your fault the soda was dumped as you should not have left it there to temp any of us girls."

"That is correct. It seemed to be the root cause of the problem, wasn't it? If I had taken the soda with me when I walked out of the office, it would not have been enticing anyone to try and get a sip."

"You are so wise, Daddy."

"If I was so wise, I would have taken the soda with me. See, we all make bad decisions, sometimes without even realizing that we are making them. The main thing is that we learn from our mistakes."

Nellie smiled at Don. "Yes. And when we learn from our mistakes, we become better kitties." Nellie looked Don straight in the eyes again. "And better humans, too."

"You are so smart, Nellie."

"I try, Daddy. Now, can you clean Billie up?"

"Only if you don't mind. I mean, I remember when you swatted my hand away when I was fluffing Billie up a while back."

"That was because I didn't know what you were doing. Now, I do."

"I'm only picking on you, buddy. I'm glad you and Billie get along so great. Alec would be so happy to know this." Don picked Nellie up and gave her a huge hug. "Well, that's different."

"What's different?"

"It sounds like you have two hearts beating inside of you."

"Well, I do prance to the beat of a different drummer."

Don laughed. "Smarty pants. OK, Neil Peart, let's go clean up Billie and then I'll get your sisters together and we can have a talk about this matter."

"I love you, Daddy."

"I love you, too, Nellie."

***

MEW 25

It was noon and Don had the house to himself until Gloria and the girls, along with Ted-D of course, all got up. Waiting for his coffee to finish being made, Don decided he would go outside and listen to the geese honk in the distance. Yes, it was fall. The leaves on the trees had already begun changing their outfits from the greens of summer to the oranges, reds, and yellows of fall. It was a beautiful time of year.

Turning from the brew master, coffee in hand, Don was met with a, well, I suppose you could say, a roar. He looked in the direction from whence it came and spied on Boo-Boo near the hallway looking up at him.

"Well, look who's up? Boo-Boo! Did you have sweet dreams?"

"Yes, I did, Daddy. Did you?"

"I guess you could say I did. At least I didn't wake up screaming."

Boo-Boo laughed. "Good thing, Daddy, otherwise I believe the rest of us would have done the same."

Don smiled, took a sip of his coffee and bent down to give Boo-Boo a pet. "Well, I was just about to head outside and do a little bit more waking up. How about yourself?"

"Daddy, you know what time it is."

"Yes, it's noon."

"Not only that, but it's time for me to sing a song."

"Oh my gosh. How could I have forgotten about that? Why of course it is."

Following Boo-Boo to her room, Don put his coffee down on the dresser and began scratching the top post. Boo-Boo took her claws and scratched at the bottom post then took to the top ledge, the stage.

"All warmed up, Boo-Boo?"

"Yes, Daddy. Are you ready for a song?"

"Why, of course I am. Best way to start the day is with my little singer singing one of her greatest hits."

"Oh, Daddy. Ok, here I go." And with that, Boo-Boo began noodling on the stage. Yes, noodling. When Boo-Boo sings, she noodles away at the material, and with her paws, she will stretch out her toes and grab a finger which I offer her. Don't worry, it is attached to my hand.

Boo-Boo seems to outdo herself each time she sings. I find myself getting so relaxed, standing there, watching her, that I'll keep my finger within her reach for her to pull on and my head will be bowed. In peaceful relaxation.

With my finger being held with her nails, the warmth of her paw and soft pads it is like a massage, a different type of relaxation. Boo-Boo will then take her paw and begin to insert her nails ever-so-slightly into my scalp, massaging the stress out of me before my day begins.

"That feels so good. Thank you, Boo-Boo."

"You're welcome, Daddy. Did you like my song?"

"Did I? Every time you sing, you seem to only get better and better. Each song as beautiful as you are and that is very beautiful."

Boo-Boo smiled that smile only Boo-Boo can give, the ends of her mouth pulling upwards and her eyes twinkling.

"Thank you, Daddy. I practice a lot. Just like you when you go to your music room and play your sax. Practice, no matter what you are doing, can only make us better at what we do."

"Very true. Very true, my Boo-Boo." Don petted her and rubbed her ear. "Thanks again, buddy. I best get going on my day now. Love you, Boo-Boo."

"Love you, Daddy." Boo-Boo turned around and licked her butt.

***

MEW 26

"Sisters, sisters," Ted-D cried at the top of his lungs. "Hurry into the kitchen."

All four sisters came running into the kitchen. "What's going on Ted-D?" asked Marbles. "I thought we were getting treats. I do not see treats. All I see is Daddy under the sink." Marbles and the girls stared at Daddy's legs; the only thing they could really make out since his head was inside the cabinet.

"No treats, Marbles. But" Ted-D stopped for emphasis here. "But it is time for. . ."

"Yes, Ted-D, continue."

"It's time for us to jump up and down on Daddy, Marbles. All of us," Ted-D gleefully stated.

All together, the sisters agreed with Ted-D. "Oh, that does sound like fun." Before Daddy had a chance to resist, he found himself being used as a trampoline.

Ted-D hopped up on Daddy's belly, then Boo-Boo jumped off the counter, landing near Ted-D sending him in the air with a laugh that Momma could hear from the other room.

As soon as Ted-D flew up, Yogie came in to join the fun, sending Boo-Boo straight up into the sink. Then Nellie took her turn, yelling "Meow!" as she went through the air sending Yogie up into the air only to land on Daddy's face in which Daddy made a stinky face.

Not to be left out, Marbles cannon balled onto Daddy's belly and sent Nellie straight up to the ceiling fan where she grabbed ahold and made helicopter noises.

Daddy finally managed to get out from beneath the sink as Momma walked into the kitchen to see what all the shenanigans was.

"Oh, they're just having fun, Love."

"Well, it's a good thing you didn't hit your head on the pipes. I'd be looking at you having to forgo your camping trip. Then, when would my quiet time happen?"

Don laughed. "I'm not sure how much quiet time you'll be getting with these youngins' even when I am camping."

"Well, just the same, we don't need you hurt." At that moment, Boo-Boo cried out from the sink, "I'm stuck. I'm stuck."

Don got off the floor and turned towards Boo-Boo. "How are you stuck? I see each of your paws and nothing seems to be stuck."

"My tail went down the drain." Boo-Boo said.

"What? Let me look." Daddy took Boo-Boo gently in his hands and moved Boo-Boo so he could see where her tail was stuck. As he did so, Boo-Boo quickly brought it out of the drain and bopped Daddy on his noggin.

Laughing like there was no tomorrow, Momma smiled. "You girls sure have got a lot of your Daddy in you. You too, Ted-D."

"Is that a good thing, Momma?"

"Yes, I must admit it is Ted-D. Humor is a good trait to have. It makes life so much easier to enjoy, otherwise it would be too serious."

"They have grown up so much in this past year, haven't they Love?"

"Yes, they have. Just look at you girls." Boo-Boo looked at Momma and Daddy from her position in the sink, while the others did the same from their landing positions. Ted-D smiled a smile, that it looked as if it wrapped around his face and came back to join the other side under his nose.

"My sisters have learned so much since we adopted them last year, haven't they?" Ted-D said proudly.

"Yes, they have. And they could not have done it without their big brother either." Ted-D puffed out his chest. "Thank you, Momma. You make my brown blush."

"Oh, you are so cute yourself, Ted-D buddy." Daddy continued, "But your mother speaks the truth. "You have helped your sisters learn so much this past year."

"I must say, Daddy, that they have in turn taught me a lot, too."

"Together, this nucleus of a family does help one another in many positive ways, doesn't it, Love?"

"Yes, we do, Honey. Yes, we do."

"OK then, time for me to put my tools away and let you girls and Ted-D have some quiet time. I'll go up north and enjoy Mother Nature and reground."

"I'll miss you, Daddy." Nellie said as she looked down from the fan.

"Come here my Nellie buddy." Daddy reached out and helped Nellie down from the ceiling fan. Pulling Nellie close to his chest, he gave her a hug. Then he gave her another hug. "I'll be home before you know it." Then he whispered in Nellie's ear, "I'll miss you, too, buddy" and gave her another hug.

***

MEW 27

"Look, it's snowing outside," exclaimed Boo-Boo, pointing a paw toward the window. "Momma made it snow outside." Boo-Boo giggled. They all ran to the window, tumbling over one another. The flakes glistened on the ground, fresh ones falling from the Heaven's, adding more to their winter wonderland. They stared upwards in wonder as Momma got out of her van and blew each a kiss.

Staring back at them, sight unseen, in a different dimension, was Alec. Alec-the-Cat, their predecessor. She had a tear in her eye as she watched the kittens enjoying themselves.

Around the corner, Marvin-the-Cat, Alec's predecessor, appeared. "It does pain the heart at times, does it not, Alec?"

Alec turned around, facing away from the kittens, pawed at a tear that landed on her whisker and replied, "Yes, at times, it just doesn't seem fair. I mean, Don and Gloria were my family."

"Yes, that is true, as it is also true that they were my family. Yet, time does not stop when we do. That may be why it hurts, as we never forget what it was. How good we had it when it was our turn on Earth. Yet, you must take pride in having chosen those kittens to fill the void you left behind. Not an easy task since you were, I mean, are special. I went through the same thing many, many years ago. Unlike you, though, I could not find a kitten or four to take my place. Not for many years. Then you came along."

Alec smiled at Marvin's words. "Thank you, Marvin, for allowing me a good home."

"It is I who thank you, Alec. You have made our humans very happy. Now Nellie, Boo-Boo, Marbles, and Yogie will take over from where you left off. And the extra special attention you gave Nellie?" Alec looked up in apprehension as Marvin continued, "You left a piece of you in her to help Don transition, too." Marvin smiled.

"Thank you." Alec looked down at Nellie and purred.

Through something we humans will never understand, yet the feline world does, Nellie looked up, purring, and smiled back.

Turning to face Marvin again, Alec asked, "What happens now? If you are still here, I take it that I may always be here, too?"

"Come with me, Alec."

Alec followed Marvin to the golden, catnipped scratching post. Extending nails, Marvin began scratching, his nails slowly tugging at the golden threads. "Join me."

"Join you?" Alec asked, puzzled.

Looking directly at Alec, Marvin nodded.

"Alone, one is never too smart. Let us now learn together."

***

Thank you for reading our story. We hope you like it and will tell others about us. We also hope you read our first book, "*When You Hear Meow.*" That is the book that began our journey.

~ Boo-Boo, Nellie, Marbles, Yogie, and Ted-D (with Billie and Alec-the-Cat.) RIP buddy, RIP.

(Upper left, upper right, bottom right, bottom left, and center.)

Alec Gould. Com

www.ingramcontent.com/pod-product-compliance
Lightning Source LLC
Chambersburg PA
CBHW060357080526
44583CB00012B/354